The Golden Book of
JEWISH HUMOR

Harry Golden's other books:

The Golden Book
of
JEWISH
HUMOR

by HARRY GOLDEN

G. P. Putnam's Sons
New York

Copyright © 1972 by Harry Golden

N. C.
808.7
Gc

a. 2.

Dedicated to the memory of two beloved friends:
  Harry Lang, longtime Sunday editor of the JEWISH
  DAILY FORWARD,
  and
  L. Wolfe Gilbert, songwriter, "Waitin' for the
  Robert E. Lee" and a thousand other songs.
  Both men of good humor.

Contents

Acknowledgments

A BOOK of this kind must draw from many sources. I have leaned heavily on my own writings which have appeared in more than twenty years' issues of the *Carolina Israelite*. In addition, I've drawn from some of my books, in particular, *Only in America* (1958); *For 2¢ Plain* (1959); *Enjoy, Enjoy* (1960); *You're Entitle'* (1962); *So What Else Is New?* (1964); *Ess, Ess, Mein Kindt* (1966); and *So Long as You're Healthy* (1970).

I've utilized some stories from that fine little book by Immanuel Olsvanger *Royte Pomerantsen* (Schocken Books, 1965). The stories from that volume reprinted here are indicated with an (*) and were translated for the present collection by Joel Waxman of New York. Mr. Waxman also translated some stories for me from *The Treasures of Jewish Humor* by Rabbi Isaac Ashkenazi, published by Tel Aviv Publishers (1929), indicated herewith by (**). From Leo Rosten's incomparable book *The Joys of Yiddish* (McGraw-Hill Publishing Company, 1968), I have selected some stories that are memorable. Also, I have drawn from *Jewish Wit* by Theodor Reik (Taplinger, 1966); *The Fireside Treasury of Modern Humor* by Scott Meredith (Simon & Schuster, 1963), *Tales from the Bagel Lancers* by Jerry Blumenfeld (The World Publishing Company), and *Encyclopedia of Jewish Humor* edited by Henry D. Spalding (Jonathan David

Publishers, 1969). Grateful thanks are hereby expressed to the authors, editors, and publishers, without whom this book could not have been compiled. My article, "God Bless the Gentile," originally appeared in *Playboy* Magazine, copyright 1966 by HMH Publishing Company, Inc. Finally, many of the best stories here are through the courtesy of Anonymous, the world's most prolific author.

HARRY GOLDEN

Introduction

BEFORE I wrote my first book, I knew two jokes. One was: Who was that lady I saw you with last night; and the other one wasn't.

I stared out my window. I saw three men on the street corner. I remembered. One Jew on the street corner is overcoming all history. Two Jews are a cabal. Three Jews on the street corner are wondering why a fourth doesn't give more to charity.

Jewish humor comes from different neighborhoods.

Probably all humor at its core expresses the same three or four or five and six sentiments. The playwright Euripides said, "Write the promises of women on water," and two centuries later, the American journalist and politician Boise Penrose advised his lovelorn: "Never write a letter to a woman you can't cool a beer on."

One of the best ways to understand a people is to know what makes them laugh. Laughter encompasses the limits of the soul. In humor life is redefined and accepted. Irony and satire provide much keener insights into a people's collective psyche and values than do years of research.

People have little sympathy with stolidity. Dick Gregory was most effective when he introduced humor into the civil rights struggle.

My own Golden Vertical Negro Plan broke the ice as it were. The Plan was the first "integrationist" story which appeared in the newspapers of the Deep South. They could not afford not to print it.

Humor has been so much a part of the Jewish culture that any kind of activity at all is impossible without it. The Jews are brought together by sharing humor of their past. The more desperate the problem the more humor is directed to describe it.

At the core of Jewish humor is the belief that God made it hard to be a Jew for His own reasons. It is even harder than He imagined because the world is filled with Gentiles.

Much of our humor is "black humor," the Yiddish humor originally conceived in the *shtetl* and in the ghetto of the Russian Pale of Settlement. "Pale" means "fence," and the Pale of Settlement extended across a third of Russia. Millions of non-Jews lived within this prescribed area, but the Jews were restricted by the czars to their *shtetl*, a hamlet populated only by Jews. In the cities within the Pale, in Odessa, Kishinev, Kovno, Lodz, Jews were confined to the ghetto, a prison community. Here they suffered through pogroms, incursions by the Cossacks, and dire poverty.

Despite these misadventures, Jews developed their own economy and their own trades; their own schools, which they called yeshivas; and their own language, Yiddish, originally a German dialect spelled with Hebrew letters which, over the years, not only accumulated scores of Polish, Russian, and Lithuanian words, but which spawned its own dialects. It was a language the fancy uptown German Jews of New York City later called "jargon."

12

Introduction

In their *shtetlach* and ghettos, the Jews honed and refined Yiddish, made it a viable language which inspired a bitter humor describing their despair.

"God helps those who help themselves," says the optimistic Christian.

"God gave us shoulders," says the Jew, "and he gave us burdens."

All men worry about survival, but the Jewish view is that survival is not always up to the individual. There are few homilies in Yiddish—which is what lent its humor bite. Yiddish is one of the few effects the East European Jews brought with them when they started to come to America in the 1880's.

Out of Yiddish came a reputable theater, a press, and a literature. Yiddish has, of course, waned with the passing of the immigrant generation. There is still a Yiddish theater in New York City, but the actors and the audience have grown old together. And there is still a Yiddish press which yearly loses money, a loss the publishers shrug off by saying, "A man has got to make a living somehow."

But the literature survives, particularly the stories of Sholom Aleichem, and not forgetting Isaac Bashevis Singer, one of the preeminent modern writers who, sophisticated New Yorker though he is, still writes his short stories in Yiddish which are subsequently translated into English, French, German, and even Hebrew.

Neither these writers nor the others—I. L. Peretz, Abraham Reisen, or H. Leivick—ever invested Yiddish with the range of possibilities with which Chaucer and Shakespeare invested English or Homer and Plato Greek. Yiddish was a community endeavor, a pessimistic community which, instead of being dour and ascetic, was humorous and mystical.

Sholom Aleichem writes about the people in this community whose heads God screwed on left-handed. Some of them, like Tevye, the dairyman, hold long conversations with God. A lengthy conversation with God is no newer than the Book of Job and certainly, to borrow from the Latin, a sinister God screwed on Don Quixote's head.

Where Don Quixote wanted to change the world for the better, Tevye wants only to live with dignity in his *shtetl,* both impossible tasks. Where Job finally realizes he cannot comprehend the vastness of God, Tevye talks to Him as though He were an unreasonable landlord.

Sholom Aleichem is the *meshugganah* joke raised to literature. The *meshugannah* joke concerns the immigrant peddler who, at the height of the nighttime rush hour, keeps searching for something on each corner of Forty-second Street until the cop walks over and asks what's the matter.

"I lost a twenty-dollar bill," says the peddler.

"On which corner do you think you lost it?" asks the cop.

"I didn't lose it on Forty-second Street. I lost it on Twenty-third Street, but there's more light here."

The *shtetlach* of Isaac Bashevis Singer are populated with the same *meshugahim,* but they must also contend with demons and devils. The critic Irving Howe believes the animating principle behind Singer's work is "anti-Promethean, a disbelief in the efficacy of striving, defiance, and pride, a doubt as to the sufficiency of knowledge or even wisdom."

Introduction

Isaac Bashevis Singer's joke is about the hostile world raised to literature.

Two Jews walk through a menacing neighborhood at night. Ahead, they see two toughs. "Let's run," says one Jew to the other. "There are two of them and we are alone."

Singer and Sholom Aleichem played an instrumental role in the qualitative effects of the Yiddish joke. If they hadn't written, Yiddish jokes would not be as incisive as they are.

And Yiddish itself still plays a creative role in the Jewish joke about America. The thrust of the Jewish immigrant was toward assimilation, toward becoming an unbearded, blue-eyed, blond American. The jokes about this effort to adapt revealed the difficulty and often the futility of the process. The Yiddish word or phrase on which the joke depended was a reminder of the teller's origins.

Immigrant Jews understood they were unlettered, innocent, and naïve. They were greenhorns and they made jokes about their naïveté. One of these, a genuine chestnut, which circulated through the tenements of the Lower East Side when I was a boy, still has currency.

An immigrant housewife explains to her neighbor her husband doesn't feel well because the doctor says he has a cancer.

"Cancer-schmancer," says the neighbor, *"abee gezundt!"* *

There were, to be sure, jokes beyond number about the pretensions of the newcomers to rise in their new

---

* "So long as he's healthy!"

15

country, the most interesting of which centered on the black man. The hope of the black man and the Jew for equality and acceptance by the white middle class was equally intense, but the Jewish expectation was higher. So the black man became a surrogate Jew for the immigrants, a warning that pretension did not conceal beginnings. These were cruel jokes, perhaps to ease the realization that the joke about the black man was finally a mocking joke about Jewish hopes and expectations.

The telephone rings. "No, Mr. Greenbaum is not here. He's at his business club. No, Mrs. Greenbaum is not here either. She's at the Hilton in Miami Beach. No, Cissy Greenbaum is at the Junior League. No, Sonny Greenbaum is at Harvard. Who dis? Dis the *shvartze*." *

Another joke describes the anguish of two black porters working at a Catskill resort. They are overjoyed at the prospects of their summer employment and dream together of the extravagant tips they will collect because the Jews have all the money. They collect no tips the first week and begin to worry that it may be true Jews are all Shylocks; they get less the second week and agree the Jews are undermining the economy; at the end of the third week, they agree that the Jews killed Christ.

On Labor Day, all the husbands appear to transport their families home and lavish $10 and $25 tips on the two men for their summer services.

Meeting later, one porter says to the other, "We wuz wrong. The Jews didn't kill Christ."

"They just worried him to death," says the partner.

* *Shvartze* = black—colored maid.

A joke I must quote re-creates the dialogue between two black menservants.

"Ah work for a fine Jewish fambly. Very religious. They keep the Yom Kippur."

"Ah work for a Jewish fambly, too. Dey keep the Shabbas."

"Shabbas? What am de Shabbas?"

"Why, man, Yom Kippur am *dreck* to de Shabbas."

When assimilation became the secure condition of American Jewry, the jokes changed. There is still a concern with the black man, but immodestly I suggest my Vertical Negro Plan is at a far remove from the jokes my father told about blacks, and Norman Podhoretz's essay "My Negro Problem—And Ours" is probably at a far remove from his father's analysis. When, in fact, Jews make jokes about blacks today, the jokes differ in neither finesse or subtlety from the jokes told by segregationists.

Some of the old Yiddish jokes in dialect still make the rounds because they still afford instant drama. Here is the dialogue between Abe and Becky on the night before their wedding: (the teller provides the dialect!)

"Do it with me tonight, Becky."

"No, Abe, I can't."

"Give me three good reasons why you can't."

"First, Abe, if I did it, you wouldn't marry me. Two, when your mother came to look at the sheets, it wouldn't be there. And three, doing it gives me a headache."

With assimilation, the stage Jew disappeared. The stage Jew was the invention of the Gentiles. He was Shylock without Jessica. The Jewish writer Leslie Fiedler

17

points out that in the beginning the Jews the Gentiles created were far more real than those created by the Jews. The fictional characters of Sidney Luska, Ludwig Lewisohn, Abe Cahan, and Ben Hecht were irrelevant to the facts of the American experience, while Hemingway's Robert Cohn of *The Sun Also Rises,* an accident, says Fiedler, of Hemingway's anti-Semitic malice, was not.

Once Jews had fully participated in the American experience and began to re-create it, they gave Shylock back his daughter, and the jokes they told were about Jewish traveling salesmen.

The Jewish jokes now, fortunately or unfortunately, are coined by the stand-up or nightclub comedian. The Jews saw a good thing in Will Rogers and W. C. Fields, entertainers who could do it all alone before an audience. But they had to wait until other Jews made enough money to frequent nightclubs and theaters.

There were Jewish comedians in vaudeville, but they usually worked as part of a team—Weber and Fields come to mind and Gallagher and Shean. There were also Jewish comedians only incidentally Jewish. Jack Benny started as a "red tie" comedian making fun of effeminacy in tandem with Mary Livingstone, and George Burns was the straight man for the droll wit of Irish Gracie Allen.

Georgie Jessel and Joe E. Lewis depended upon the Jewish milieu to give their jokes crispness and immediacy. Sophie Tucker and Fannie Brice were Jews. And you don't have to be Jewish to laugh at the jokes of Mort Sahl, Paul Krassner, or Shelley Berman; you only have to understand what *cover charge* means.

The apotheosis of the stand-up comedian was Lenny

Bruce, whose drug addiction, politicizing, and scatological language outraged us in the late 1950's. There isn't a disc jockey today, however, who doesn't ape Lenny Bruce although the disc jockeys carefully edit him.

The most successful and popular of the stand-up comedians is Bob Hope. I think he is successful in some measure because one doesn't have to be an urban sophisticate to laugh at his wisecracks. His wide appeal to the middle class comes perhaps because he is the comedian talking about Wondercup bread while the rest are singing the praises of Jewish rye.

The mechanics of the Jewish joke have passed now into the American canon. Madison Avenue ad men have discovered the Jewish mother and installed her as a heroine in commercials more tasteless than those for deodorants. I heard a Gastonia traffic court judge, a bone-of-the-bone, blood-of-the-blood Southerner, address a defendant with: "What are you? One of those cockamamie Sunday drivers?" and the last Jewish joke I heard was about the Lone Ranger and Tonto who were surrounded by howling Apaches.

"It looks like we're done for," says the Lone Ranger.

"Where do you get that 'we' shit, white man?" asks Tonto.

Next to discovering the source of the Nile, the hardest search is to discover who first wrote the joke that is currently making the circuit.

I once invented a joke. At least, I believe I invented it, but then you never know. Maybe I did hear it someplace first. At any rate, I was in serious discussion with an agent who is housed in the largest and most famous agency in the world—on Madison Avenue. The place runs rampant with wall-to-wall carpeting and wood paneling, and even the elevators are air-conditioned.

All the men who work at this huge agency are crisply perfect in their dress. No one can tie a necktie knot like a member of this agency. It is the smallest knot in the world.

Looking around at the ostentatious good taste of the room, I told the agent, apropos of nothing, that each office in the agency ought to have a sign similar to the famous THINK sign invented by Thomas Watson of IBM. Only the agency sign should read:

> DRESS BRITISH
>
> THINK YIDDISH

Visiting in Detroit three days later, I met a press agent for Twentieth Century-Fox who asked, "Have you heard the latest? Dress British, Think Yiddish."

The next night I was on a midnight radio program in New York. A good friend of mine who handles press relations for a famous motion-picture producer was there. He got us all in a huddle and said, "Have you heard the latest?" And here it was again.

I think I invented this joke, but in a matter of days I heard it from all parts of the country. This leads me to conclude that jokes are concocted by some sort of spontaneous combustion, like folk songs, or that the agent indeed followed my advice and had the sign hung that said:

> DRESS BRITISH
>
> THINK YIDDISH

The Whole World Is Jewish

S ARA LIPSHITZ, a buxom blonde, wore at a charity ball, an enormous diamond.

"It happens to be the third most famous diamond in the whole world," she boasted. "The first is the Hope diamond, then comes the Kohinoor, and then comes this one, which is called the Lipshitz."

"What a diamond!"

"How lucky you are!"

"Wait, wait, what luck? Nothing in life is all *mazel*," said Sara, the diamonded dame. "Unfortunately, with this famous Lipshitz diamond you must take the famous Lipshitz curse!"

The ladies buzzed and tsked. "And what's the Lipshitz curse?"

"Lipshitz," sighed the lady.

🌷 🌷 🌷

Mournfully, Mr. Lefkowitz entered the offices of his burial society. "I've come to make the funeral arrangements for my dear wife."

"Your wife?" asked the astonished secretary. "But we buried her last year!"

"That was my first wife," sighed lugubrious Lefkowitz. "I'm talking about my second."

"Second? I didn't know you remarried. *Mazel tov!*"

(Leo Rosten)

🌺 🌺 🌺

The young mother, Molly Gold, was sending her son to school for the first time.

"And Bubala, be sure you say 'yes, ma'am' when your teacher talks to you. And, Bubala, always say 'thank you' when someone gives you a present." She paused. "Bubala, I'm so excited—this is your first day at school. Bubala, be sure you remember your manners, and when you come home, Bubala, you must tell me everything you learned. Don't forget anything, Bubala. Good-bye, Bubala." Molly's farewell was tearful.

When he returned from school that afternoon, Molly was beside herself with curiosity.

"So, Bubala, tell me, what did you learn today?"

"Mama, I learned that my name is Irving," said her son.

🌺 🌺 🌺

Two old friends from the Bronx met after a period of almost ten years.

The Whole World Is Jewish

"Tell me, Tsipkah, you look fine, but aren't you shorter than when I saw you last?"

"Yes, yes, it's true; I'm shrinking."

"Shrinking! My heavens—what does the doctor say?"

"The doctor says—you should excuse the language—I'm 'an atavistic throwback.' "

Her friend stared at her for a minute, then said, "So what else is new?"

❀ ❀ ❀

The same Jewish women met in a Bronx A&P store:

"You heard maybe about the euceminik?"

"No, what's the euceminik?"

"Euceminik, that's over in Rome, the Pope he says we didn't do it."

"We didn't do what?"

"You know, the fellow on the cross with the nails and the blood."

"We didn't do it, so who done it?"

"Who done it? The Puerto Ricans, of course."

❀ ❀ ❀

Chaim Goldberg came home from his factory exhausted. It was one of those days—everything had gone wrong.

Zelda greeted him with a cheery smile. She was all

dressed up. Her best earrings were glowing, and her hair never looked better.

"Darling," she said as she greeted him. "How would you like a nice cold double martini? Then a T-bone steak and beefsteak tomatoes, with a baked potato. Then some hot apple pie with cheese." She smiled and said, "Whaddya say?"

"Not tonight, Zelda." Chaim sighed. "Let's eat home. I'm tired."

❀ ❀ ❀

The three partners were cavorting in Miami Beach. They all had decided to take a vacation together.

Suddenly Hymie clutches his head and shouts. "Oy, I forgot to lock the safe in the office."

"So what's to worry?" replied one of his partners. "We're all here, no?"

❀ ❀ ❀

Sam heard the great news, that his old friend Goldfarb had just come into a fortune. He quickly telephoned him, congratulated him, then said, "How about a little loan, say fifty dollars?"

"Nothing doing," replied Goldfarb.

"Ah," said Sam, "no one can say success has changed you."

The Jewish wedding has deep roots in history. One of the questions all Jews have to answer is: "In how many days did the Holy One, blessed be He, create the universe?"

The student answers, "In six days did He create the universe."

"And what has He been doing since then, up to now?"

And the answer, the only answer is: "Since then He has been arranging marriages."

God is a maker of marriages, but I wonder if He would bother to come to some of the affairs He has arranged.

🕎 🕎 🕎

An aging Jew, crossing the street in front of a church, was knocked down by a hit-and-run driver. As he lay there, half-conscious, a priest hurried out, knelt, and prepared to administer the last rites. "Do you believe in God the Father, God the Son, and God the Holy Ghost?"

Cried the old man, "I'm dying and he asks me riddles."

🕎 🕎 🕎

Is it accidental that the Düsseldorf Jew Heinrich Heine wrote the ballad "The Lorelei" which was so typically German that the Nazis denied Heine's authorship and declared it a national song? Is it accidental that the Jew Jacques Offenbach from Cologne on the Rhine, composed, when he was transplanted to Paris, typical French music and created the *genre canaille?* Some of the music of Gustav Mahler—for instance, the dance tunes from his Fourth Symphony—is characteristically Viennese. The waltzes of the Jews Leo Fall, Oskar Straus, Edmund Eysler, Emmerich Kalman, etc., are genuinely Viennese, and a Jew composed one of the most popular Viennese song hits, the "Fiaker-lied."

George Gershwin captured and expressed in his music the color and rhythm of the American scene, the scent and even the characteristic mental slant of the American people. An example of this quality is found in his *An American in Paris.* Equally typical in its Americanism is his campaign song from *Of Thee I Sing.* In 1924 he produced his famous *Rhapsody in Blue,* and until his death, thirteen years later, Gershwin advanced steadily in musicianship, an accruing and mastery of form, a consummate skill in symphonic orchestration, and a more sustained power of expression, until finally *Porgy and Bess* explained every aspect of Gershwin's genius.

The point I would like to make and to drive home is the following: Many of the Jewish jokes assume the local color and flavor of the countries of their origin to such an extent that they are often called typical of Berlin, Vienna, Paris, and New York without, however, entirely losing their Jewish character. The result of such an assimilatory and absorbing process is then a German-Jewish, French-Jewish, or American-Jewish compound made of two or more substances.

The Whole World Is Jewish

The Jews represent the most and the least of every culture in which they've lived and every gradation between the extremes. The *most* patriotic and the least. The *most* conservative and the *most* radical, the most *pious* and the least religious.

🏵 🏵 🏵

There's a true story of two brothers who left Warsaw, Poland, to seek their fortune in Berlin.

When they were in Berlin for a day or two, Abe said to his brother, "Simon, I think I'll go on to Paris. Lend me fifty marks for the fare."

A year went by; Simon never heard from Abe. Simon got a job in an export house and was doing pretty well as a clerk, but through the grapevine Simon learned that Abe had done very well in Paris as a land speculator. In fact, Abe became very wealthy, and never once did he send his brother the fifty marks he borrowed or even send him as much as a postcard.

After several years Simon decided to visit his wealthy brother in Paris. When he arrived there, he went to the beautiful mansion in which Abe lived and finally confronted his brother. "Abe, you're doing very well here in Paris, and I am just a clerk in Berlin. The least you could have done was send me the fifty marks you borrowed."

Abe lifted himself up to his full height of five feet three inches and said, "And not a cent will you Germans get until we get back Alsace-Lorraine!"

People who worry if their children are well and thriving are Jewish.

People who beam when you mention grandchildren are Jewish.

People who see to it that no one goes hungry or without a place to stay or a start in life are Jewish.

People who love with a passion and grow incoherent in the face of great injustice are Jewish.

People who have suffered through generations of misfortune and still love life are Jewish.

People who work hard, earn money, and spend it with great pleasure are Jewish.

People who have a talent for singing and laughing and studying and serving mankind are Jewish.

People who hope for peace and have a deep gentleness are Jewish.

People who can grow indignant and fight back are Jewish.

People who love to talk and crave company most of the time are Jewish.

This is not to say that there are no mean ones, no selfish, dishonest, or step-on-the-other-guy sorts of Jews.

Just that Jewish ideals, Jewish joys and tears, Jewish hopes for the future may be found in the hearts of all men in all places.

But particularly Jews have the gift of laughter and self-satire. Funny stories of all sorts have been a tradition and an effective aid to survival through generations of Jewish experience. A wisecrack, a barbed remark, a joke

on oneself or on the other guy—this makes the difference
between an outlook fed by gloom and despair and one
that is marked by human spirit and a hope for tomorrow.
I hope the stories that follow illustrate in some small way
this principle.

You Never Saw a Yenkee?

COMPARING the modern fund raiser to the old-fashioned *meshullach* would be like comparing a member of the New York Stock Exchange to an itinerant peddler.

The *meshullach* (agent or deputy sent by accredited Jewish institutions to collect funds) was a very hard worker and a colorful character. He would walk the streets calling on his old contacts and forever looking for new leads.

He has now practically disappeared from the scene, and in some ways it is a pity.

Invariably he wore the long caftan-type coat and a broad-brimmed black hat which made a fitting frame for his wide, untrimmed beard.

His pockets were always bulging—on one side, his papers, receipts, and notebooks, and in the other, a package with slices of bread and the usual hard-boiled eggs. This was an emergency ration in case he couldn't find the synagogue sexton or if the president of the *shul* was out of town; then the *meshullach* could take his lunch without worrying about eating nonkosher food somewhere.

The *meshullach* was probably the subject of the original story about the time that the man got off at the Southern Railroad station in a small Georgia town, and a few kids hanging around were fascinated by his garb, his beard, his bulging pockets, and his umbrella, and they proceeded to follow him down the street. Suddenly the old gent turned around and said to the kids, "What's the matter, you never saw a Yenkee?"

🌼 🌼 🌼

On the veranda of a Miami Beach hotel, Mrs. Lefkowitz was boasting to her new friend. "What a husband I got, such a sweetheart. So thoughtful. To tell you the truth, we are always holding hands, even now after twenty years of marriage."

Her friend looked admiration. "Unbelievable."

Mrs. Lefkowitz turned and looked over her shoulder. Then she added, "A good thing we do or we'd be killing each other."

🌼 🌼 🌼

The two wives were commiserating with each other over the back fence in the Bronx. Each had a son and daughter of marriageable age—but no marriage in sight.

"If only my Mortie would get married already. Thirty years old and still no wife."

"Don't worry, Sadie," said her neighbor. "Wait until the wrong girl comes along."

You Never Saw a Yenkee?

🌱 🌱 🌱

Dr. Sigmund Herskovits, the Park Avenue psychiatrist, was interviewing a new patient.

"Please tell me in simple language, what is bothering you? Do you hear voices? Are you being followed?"

"No, Doctor, I just keep wanting to open windows and jump out."

"Ah," said the doctor, "suicidal." He buzzed for his secretary and said, "Mr. Luftmentsch, my new patient, will be required to pay in advance."

🌱 🌱 🌱

"You still got an eye on the girls," said Max to his partner, Moe. "Already sixty-eight and still pinching *tochuses.*"

Moe smiled appreciatively. "Yeah"—he sighed—"but now when I chase my secretary around the desk, I walk."

🌱 🌱 🌱

Mrs. Finkel was hanging out the wash when her gossipy neighbor approached. "I hate to tell you this," said the gossip, "but there's a rumor that your husband chases girls. And at his age, too," she clucked. "He's sixty-five, no?"

"Yes, he's sixty-five," said Mrs. Finkel. "So let him

37

chase girls. Dogs chase cars also. But when they catch one, can they drive it?"

※ ※ ※

When Rabbi Harold Metzger was eighty-one years old, he was asked how he managed to maintain his health, vitality, and slim figure. "You never exercise," he was told. "All you do is pore over books without giving your muscles a chance to stay in shape."

"Oh, I stretch my muscles occasionally." The rabbi chuckled. "I get all the exercise I need acting as a pallbearer for those in my congregation who exercised!"

※ ※ ※

"Hello, Abe, how's the law business?"

"Don't even ask! It's been so long since I had a client I divorced my wife last month just so I would have a case."

(**)

※ ※ ※

In a small town in the Deep South, the Jewish community of about twenty-five families organized a congregation and made plans to build a temple.

You Never Saw a Yenkee?

The Christians of the town were enthusiastic. In addition, the Methodist minister offered the use of his church for Friday-evening Sabbath services until the temple was constructed. The Jewish members were grateful and began to use the beautiful Methodist church for their Sabbath services. One of the laymen, with considerable learning, acted as reader, and once a month or so, a visiting rabbi occupied the pulpit. The Methodist minister personally appeared every Friday evening to open the church, turn on the lights, and greet each of the Jews with "Good Shabbas."

About the third or fourth Friday evening, the Methodist minister took a seat in the rear of the church, picked up a Jewish prayer book, and participated in the service. In a matter of weeks he became a "regular" and an honored guest. After about five or six weeks of this, the Jewish members began to show a little nervousness. During the week, the Methodist would stick his head in one of the stores and in perfectly good humor call out, "Joe, you weren't at services last Friday." Joe smiled, but his heart wasn't in it. Thus under the watchful eye of the Methodist minister, the Jewish congregation achieved 100 percent attendance every single Friday. Even when a fellow was out of town or actually sick in bed, he made sure that the reader made the announcement from the pulpit. "Joe Landberg could not attend services tonight—he is in New York on a buying trip. He'll be back Tuesday." And you could bet he'd be there the following Friday night—early. But that is not the end of the story. As I witnessed the next development, I did not know whether to cry or laugh.

Along about April it gets very hot in that town. Most of the folks have cabins at the beach. The wife and children go down early in the week, and the husband joins them Friday afternoon. The temperature begins to average 94 degrees in the month of May. On Friday nights it is always 5 degrees hotter. What to do? Who would tell him? Finally a couple of fellows took the bull by the horns. "Dr. ———, we have imposed on you long enough. We have met in your beautiful church for six months now. Enough is enough. You have been too kind."

"But your temple is not yet finished," said the Methodist. But the Jews would have none of it.

"No, Doctor, until our temple is finished, we'll meet in our several homes."

The Methodist appeared to be a bit downcast, but everything seemed all right. On Sunday the Methodist asked his board of stewards to remain after services for a special meeting He said, "Look, gentlemen, the Jewish temple is only half-finished, but the members feel they have imposed on us too much. Up till now they have been meeting here on my personal invitation. Let us make it official church business. That should make them feel better."

On the following Wednesday the weekly paper carried the good news. The stewards officially offered the use of the church until such time as the temple was ready for use. The news, of course, came like a bolt out of the blue, and for the next few days the twenty-five Jews kept walking back and forth to see what progress was being made on the new construction. But they weren't even working on the roof yet.

For Rosh Hashanah the temple will be ready, but nowhere else in the country will a congregation match the attendance record during July and August of this small congregation in the Deep South.

❦ ❦ ❦

A beggar carrying a purse with money stopped over in a small town to spend the Sabbath. He left the money with the rabbi over the Sabbath. When the rabbi went to put it away, it fell from his hand and a large amount of money fell out. The rabbi immediately called a group of his most trusted friends together to decide what to do. All in all there were 1,500 rubles in the purse. Such a man has to go begging! When the beggar went to pick up the purse, he was told that he must either open a business or forfeit the money. He thought for a moment and decided to let the community keep the money because after all, he was still making a living.

(*)

❦ ❦ ❦

Beryl met Shmeryl and asked how he was getting along with his wife. Thank G-d, answered Shmeryl, "we are getting along very well. We are just like two lovebirds. We do, however, argue constantly about one thing."

"What's the big problem?" asked Beryl.

"We are always arguing about the agrarian question," was the reply.

"What's the agrarian question?" asked Beryl.

"It's like this," Shmeryl said. "I say that she should be buried in the ground, and she says that I should be buried in the ground."

(*)

❀ ❀ ❀

Auf probe, literally, "on probation," refers specifically to the trial sermon and congregational interview of a new candidate for the pulpit. "Let's go and look over the new rabbi."

If I hear of an *auf probe* anywhere within a radius of fifty miles, I am off like a fireman. There is no event in our culture which is so rich in human interest.

In the old days the rabbi had a cinch. If he could keep in the good graces of the president of the congregation, he was in like Flynn. For all I know this may still be true in some of the congregations of the metropolitan centers. But down South it is an entirely different matter. In fact there was never a time when *one man* made the decisions in the congregations of Dixie, and the reason was economics rather than democracy. In the large cities you have many strata of society within a single organization. There are manufacturers, bankers, white-collar workers, and workmen, and the few men at the top quite naturally step into their proper positions of leadership. But in the South, we represent, in the main, a single proprietary class. What we really have here are congregations composed almost exclusively of medicine men and no Indians —with practically every member qualified to sit on the dais.

Just imagine what that means for a rabbi.

The interesting fact about all this is that it parallels that religiosocial life of the Gentile community, particularly the Baptists and Methodists, who enjoy autonomy in their individual churches. In fact, one of the outstanding Baptist clergymen told me that the best way to retain a pulpit is to make a simple statement at the first interview. "Gentlemen of the board, I am the transient here and you are the permanents; tell me how you want it done, and I will do it."

Another parallel is concerned with the actual mechanics of asking a clergyman to resign his pulpit, when the "leaders" feel that he has not met their requirements. The leaders know they must act quickly—within a year or, at most, two years. Once the rabbi or Protestant minister occupies the pulpit for three or four years, the leaders have lost their initiative. They can only keep praying that the man gets a call from another congregation. The reason for this is that the majority of the congregation is not at all close to the internal management of the organization. Since they do not attend services regularly, the rabbi or Protestant minister is that fine fellow who sends them an interesting bulletin every week, and they are all for him. Should the leaders call a congregational meeting for the purpose of replacing the clergyman, the majority will nearly always uphold him. Another factor of course is the natural tendency to vote "against the machine," irrespective of the issues involved. The leaders understand this. If they do not like a rabbi, they know they must act quickly.

The *auf probe* session therefore is full of tension and drama. The leaders are under great pressure, especially if they have already decided to take the new fellow. In such cases they must be very careful in the conduct of the meeting. Being a leader is not all beer and skittles.

The new rabbi is under pressure, too. What to give them? He wonders why they let the other fellow go. Of course he could use the sermon he wrote for his graduation from the seminary. But that doesn't go anymore. He tries to feel his way to see if he can find a clue. What to emphasize? Community chest activities? Rotary work? Adult education? Interfaith? Sunday school? Mr. and Mrs. Club? The *auf probe* rabbi usually takes the intelligent course and comes through with a sermon on the Biblical portion of the week. There is one thing, however, which he does know: In most of the Protestant churches and Jewish temples of the South today, the leaders are emphasizing one thing very strong: "Stick to religion—only."

After the trial sermon there may be some questions from the floor, and this part of the *auf probe* session reflects, I think, our most interesting characteristic—ambivalence. It is natural that the folks would like to have a handsome rabbi. On this basis we are no different from all the other peoples of the world. The shaman of the primitive peoples was always the tallest member of the tribe. Eventually, when we discovered the uses of intellect, we learned how to make up for lack of physical beauty by dressing him in robes, white wigs, purple togas, ermine capes, and miters. Most of the folks in the South, reflecting the attitudes of the dominant society, would like to have a rabbi (you should pardon me) who does not look "too Jewish" (as it has been so often said), yet there is much more to it than that. There is also a terrible longing for the religious and communal culture of their parents and an inherent devotion to the "glories of the past." They want a tall, blue-eyed rabbi, but they also want "a Jewish word," which is a Yiddish colloquialism for "Jewishness" in its deepest sense. What they would really like to have, of course, is Robert Montgomery with "a Jewish word."

Part of this ambivalence is in the theology itself. The members of the Reform congregation, never sure that they have done the right thing, want a rabbi with just a smattering of the Orthodox values. The Conservatives, on the other hand, want a rabbi with at least a tinge of the reformer. This often leads to the ambiguity we know so well in our American political structure: Tories who are Democrats and radicals who are Republicans.

And all during the *auf probe* the ladies are just dying to find out something about the rabbi's wife. They love to have a rabbi's wife of whom they can say, "How sweet," "How self-sacrificing," "She's such a good worker." This means, of course, that the rabbi has a homely wife, which is the ideal situation. A handsome clergyman with a homely wife can practically write his own ticket. But in the early moments of the *auf probe* the ladies do not even know whether the rabbi is married, and so the smartest of them starts the ball rolling. "Rabbah, do you-all think your wife will like it down heah?" What a brain!

And there are always the people who had been particularly fond of the "resigned" rabbi. In an attempt to demonstrate this loyalty they will make it as hard as they can for the new fellow. On the other hand, the leaders will find it necessary to go all out in their praise. Between these two extremes the new clergyman dares not hope for a smooth inauguration of his ministry.

But after a while the congregation scatters again; the

majority reads the weekly bulletin and slowly but surely transfers all past loyalties to the new man, but the leaders take up their vigil: "For the first year we want written committee reports, and please fill in the space under 'cooperation.' " Eventually the new rabbi may even ask for a raise, and the leaders sitting around the country club will shake their heads in disbelief: "What does he need an extra five hundred dollars for?" The wives will be sitting at the edge of the swimming pool and will join in: "They have such a cute little house—so neat. It's such a charming little place especially since we had those leaks fixed."

And so we'll continue along our interesting path, a dynamic people with a wonderful ambivalence. But if a rabbi in the North is looking for peace and quiet, let him not look toward the Mason-Dixon line.

🌱 🌱 🌱

The folks in North Carolina opened their hearts and their homes to the soldiers in training at Fort Bragg, the great infantry camp, which is also headquarters of the Eighty-second Airborne Division. For Thanksgiving Day in 1943, many hostesses invited soldiers for their Thanksgiving Day dinner. One very rich lady with a big home called the captain and said she could have at least three soldiers at her Thanksgiving table. "And," she said, "we're not prejudiced at all, but we'd rather not have any Jewish soldiers."

On Thanksgiving Day, her doorbell rang. Outside were three great big smiling black soldiers, and one said, "Lady, Captain Levy done sent us."

You Never Saw a Yenkee?

🕎 🕎 🕎

The late Supreme Court Justice Felix Frankfurter had a tongue that could clip a hedge. Yet he would often be quite benign with those whose ideas differed from his own. He was once asked to explain this paradox, and he gave this historic answer:

"I am *always* tolerant with those who disagree with me. After all, they have a perfect right to their ridiculous opinions."

🕎 🕎 🕎

Jake and Sadie were getting on in years, yet once a week they still went to the supermarket to shop for groceries. On one of these trips they took along little Isadore, their grandson, whom they had agreed to care for that afternoon. Pushing Isadore's perambulator up and down the aisles, Jake and Sadie soon had the baby vehicle overflowing with cereals, Cel-ray Tonic, salami, and rye bread. At the check-out counter, however, something went wrong when Jake and Sadie went back for a last-minute item.

After they had emerged from the market with the overburdened perambulator and were walking back to the apartment, Sadie suddenly gasped and put her hand on Jake's arm. "My God!" she screamed. "We've taken the wrong baby!"

Jake kept right on walking. "Keep quiet, Sadie," he told her. "This one is in a better carriage."

❀ ❀ ❀

You know what happened to me the other day? I went to the wealthiest Jew in town to ask for a donation. In the kitchen I spoke to his wife, who asked me what I wanted. I told her that I wanted to ask her husband for a donation. She became furious and really let me have it. She told me to go back where I came from. Then she left me alone in the kitchen. So I left without a donation. But what did God do? When I left the kitchen, I found a silver spoon in my pocket.

(*)

❀ ❀ ❀

One afternoon a guest came to visit a fellow Jew. The host was very happy indeed. He asked the gentleman to sit down. He then asked if he would like something to eat.

"No," replied the guest, "I've just been at the Isaacsons', and I had a fine meal. However, I would like something to nibble on."

The host brought out a chicken leg, and the guest nibbled the whole drumstick. Then he nibbled at a nice piece of potato pudding. Then he nibbled at a nice piece of flanken and a stuffed derma.

The host looked at his guest and said to him, "Listen, next time eat here, and nibble at the Isaacsons'. "

(*)

❀ ❀ ❀

You Never Saw a Yenkee?

Irving was sitting on the pot in a public pay toilet when he noticed with dismay that the roller had no toilet paper. Glancing about, Irving noticed that the adjoining booth was occupied.

"Excuse me, mister," Irving hissed. "But have you got any tissue in your booth?"

A second later the answer came back, "No—not a shred of paper in mine"

Irving thought a moment. "Well, did you by any chance bring a newspaper along with you or a magazine?"

The adjoining gentleman had to admit that he had not.

"Well, look," Irving said finally, "do you have two fives for a ten?"

🌷 🌷 🌷

In a town lived a very wealthy man who unfortunately was very stingy. He was so stingy that if you asked him what time it was, he said it was ten minutes earlier than it was. There was also a saying that whoever is not stingy will never be rich. Once a Jew came to him very late at night and asked him to teach him how to be stingy. The stingy one immediately shook hands with this fellow. The guest noticed that when he shook hands, the stingy man counted his fingers to see if there were still ten. "*Nu*," he said, "we can talk about stinginess at night also." Immediately he shut off the light and sat next to his guest. One thing was soon obvious to the guest. They sat for quite a while, and the guest learned a great deal

49

about stinginess, things he never heard before in his life. When he had to leave, he struck a match and lit a light which was on the table. When the lamp shone, it became clear that the stingy one had no pants on. The answer came quickly. "When I sit in the dark, I always take off my pants so they shouldn't wear out."

(*)

🌱 🌱 🌱

'A poor man once came to a wealthy but stingy man. He asked him for a donation. The wealthy man began to chew him out. He mocked at him as best he knew how.

The poor man became upset and said, "I only did what was right. May the one that sent me come to you."

The rich man became even angrier. "What kind of gall is that?" he demanded. "Who sent you?"

"Poverty sent me, and I hope he comes to visit you!"

(*)

🌱 🌱 🌱

Jewish jokes in print are, properly speaking, incomplete. They should really be heard and seen. Their communication is not only verbal. The gestures and the facial expressions, the rise and fall of the voice of the storyteller are essential parts of the telling. Such anecdotes are not only told, but also acted and when you speak of their language, those external factors must be considered.

☙ ☙ ☙

"Why do you Jews answer a question with another question?" a Gentile asks. "Why should we not answer with a question?" the Jew replies. This sounds comic, but as far as I know, no one has attempted to explain that Jewish peculiarity. It is easy to refer to the manner of Talmudic debates which sometimes make the impression of a game of questions, answers, and new questions. But this is no explanation; it rather begs the question.

A significant hint can perhaps be inferred from language. We speak of firing, flinging, hurling questions at someone, of embarrassing, plaguing, and vexing someone with questions, and questioning is sometimes used as synonym of grilling. In medieval time, torture was called questioning.

☙ ☙ ☙

Finky Finkelstein had suffered from mysterious pains for years. His head ached, his eyes watered, his neck was stiff, and his shoulders ached. Finky finally grew tired of eating aspirin tablets and went to see a specialist. After a thorough examination the medical man shook his head gravely and advised Finky that the source of his trouble was an extremely rare condition in which the weight of the male sexual part was so excessive as to cause pains in the upper abdomen. "We'll have to amputate," said the doctor sadly. Finky fainted away at the mere thought, but a week or so later he returned to the office and signed the permission papers so that the specialist could proceed with the operation. His aches and pains had become too much to bear.

A month later Finky was back in circulation, having decided to make the best of a rather drastic situation. The money he used to spend taking out girls, Finky thought, he could now invest in a new car, a new apartment, and a new outfit of clothes. Accordingly, he stopped by a fancy men's shop on Broadway and told the manager that he wanted a complete wardrobe—from hat to shoes. "Ho-kay," said the store manager, rubbing his hands at this opportunity to show his expertise. Looking Finky over carefully, he began an exact inventory, without benefit of tape measure. "You take a size seven and a quarter hat," he told Finky, "and a forty-two jacket." Circling around his bewildered customer, he went on, "Your shoes are nine-C width, and your shirt collar is sixteen."

Finky was amazed. "How do you know all that?" he gasped. "And all of it accurate!"

"Simple," said the manager. He had been in business for forty years, and he had never once made a mistake about measurements. "For a belt," he went on, "you wear a size thirty, and for. . . ."

But Finky had to interrupt. "You're wrong about the belt," he said with emphasis. "I have always worn a size twenty-eight!"

The shopkeeper smiled and shook his head. "I'm never wrong about things like that, my boy," he told Finky. "I would say that if you wore a size twenty-eight belt, you would probably develop headahces, watery eyes, a stiff neck, and maybe aching shoulders. . . ."

🌑 🌑 🌑

Thirty years ago if you went to Coney Island on a hot summer's day and yelled "Abie" or "Jake" through a megaphone, you could collect every lost kid on the beach. In fact, this is the way it was done. A policeman kept patrolling the boardwalk yelling "Abie" and "Jake," and the kids were found even before their parents knew they were lost. But today no kid would turn his head.

You have to yell "Scott" or "Kingston."

About the only family that still sticks by the old standbys is the British royal family. They still rely on Charles, Mary, Elizabeth, and the like. The rest of the families in Britain and America name their children Elliot, Candy, Robin, Ainsley, Brooks, Penny, or Fenimore.

There's a sort of depressing romantic sameness about them. Practically no child is named after a maiden aunt who owns three hundred shares of AT&T. Either the thrifty maiden aunt is a thing of the past, or our prosperity is so great that no one wants to curse a child with Abigail just to get three hundred shares of AT&T.

🌑 🌑 🌑

Dave Friedman, owner of Royal Furs, although a married man, was deeply infatuated with his secretary. But she couldn't stand the man.

Despite the continued rebuffs, he persisted with his unwanted attentions until one day she made her feelings perfectly clear.

"Whisper the three little words that will have me walking on air," he pleaded.

The secretary looked up and then told him:

"Go hang yourself."

☙ ☙ ☙

While the Jewish community may not approve of former mobster Mickey Cohen, the man did have a sense of humor.

"At first I was afraid that death in the electric chair might be painful," he reminisced, "until I realized that no one had ever complained."

☙ ☙ ☙

SAM: You mean to say you're married twenty-five years and your wife still looks like a newlywed?

SID: No, I said I'm married twenty-five years and my wife still *cooks* like a newlywed!

Abe was suing his wife, Sadie, for divorce, and his lawyer was determined to put her in as bad a light as possible.

"What line of work were you in before you married my client?" he asked when she was on the witness stand.

"I was a stripper in a burlesque," Sadie answered promptly.

"Aha! And do you consider that a decent occupation for a respectable lady?"

"Well, to tell the truth, I was proud of my work in comparison to what my father did for a living."

The attorney smiled, sure now that he had already won his case. "Tell the court, please, just what it was that your father did for a living. Speak up, madam!"

"He was a lawyer!" she snapped.

❀ ❀ ❀

A doctor was called to the home of a very pious Orthodox Jew who lay gravely ill.

"I'll have to examine his throat," said the doctor to the man's wife. "Bring me a spoon."

The woman, as Orthodox as her husband, faltered, and then asked haltingly, *"Milchik or flayshik?"* (Milk or meat?)

❀ ❀ ❀

Birnbaum was out walking one night when a sudden storm came up. Winds whistled down Pitkin Avenue, and heavy rains transformed the neighborhood into a disaster area in a matter of minutes. Birnbaum ran for his apartment house but slipped on the sidewalk, skidded out into the street, and sank into an open manhole. "Help! Help!" he cried above the sound of the driving rain.

A policeman stuck his head over the edge of the manhole and flashed his light into the depths below. "Hang in there, old man," said the officer. "I'll get you an ambulance."

Although Birnbaum was not seriously injured, he was taking no chances. *"First* get me a priest," he moaned. *"Then* call the ambulance."

The policeman disappeared and returned five minutes later with Father Feeny. The good father peered down the manhole and asked how he could be of service.

"Cleanse my soul!" cried Birnbaum. "I'm afraid I'm on the way to glory."

Father Feeny took out his prayer book and turned to the section on preparations for the end. "What's your name, my good man?" he called down into the darkness.

"Birnbaum!" came the answer.

The clergyman was nonplussed. "Birnbaum?" he repeated. "Shouldn't you have called for a rabbi?"

Birnbaum's reply was indignant. "Do you think I'd call out the rabbi on a night like this?"

❦ ❦ ❦

During the 1930's Samuel Leibowitz was among the most prominent judges in New York, if not the United States. One of his friends, an inveterate kibbitzer, decided to have some fun with the learned barrister.

"Judge, I hate to tell you this," he said, "but a legislative committee has voted to abolish your bench."

"Who testified against me?" demanded the outraged Leibowitz.

"Well, there was Jake Zimmerman, the banker, for one."

"What!" cried Leibowitz. "Why, he's usurious. He cheats widows and orphans out of their life savings! Who else?"

"Feldman, the contractor; he voted against you also."

"That *gonif!* He cheats the underprivileged by building slum dwellings before they even become slums. He's a disgrace to the building profession. So who else?"

The friend then mentioned a number of others who, he claimed, had testified unfavorably, while, with mounting rage, the judge denounced each as a scoundrel or worse.

Finally, the kibbitzer confessed that he had only been joking, that the committee, in fact, had unanimously praised him.

"Now why," sighed Judge Leibowitz, "did you go and make me say all those mean things against the finest group of men I know?"

🌷 🌷 🌷

One day at the bridge club, Mina Hossenpfeffer could hardly wait to tell the girls the latest joke she had heard. "There were these two Jews on the trolley car—" she began, in between hands.

Minnie Goldspritz was offended. "So why is it always two Jews?" she asked.

Mina Hossenpfeffer paused and collected her thoughts. "There were two Chinamen on the trolley car," she amended. "And when they got off, one turned to the other and said, 'So, *nu,* Ching-Dow, how's by you in the garment business?' "

🌱 🌱 🌱

Little Irving Nussberg was telling his school chums about his new bicycle. "The guy at the store wanted fifty dollars for it, and I told him that was too much."

His buddies were amused. "Did you Jew him down?" they wanted to know.

"Hell, no," Irving said, spitting on the ground for emphasis. "I acted just like you guys do. I Gentile'd him up."

🌱 🌱 🌱

There was a Jew who was so stingy that he never gave a cent to charity and never did anyone a favor. He was without mercy and pity. His wife was grieved a great deal by this trait. One week a preacher came to that town and spoke very eloquently about the qualities of mercy and pity. After the sermon the Jew came home and told his wife that he was a changed man. He promised to have mercy on all he met in the future. His wife was overjoyed and waited for the first opportunity for her husband to show himself to be a new man.

That night the weather changed, and it began to snow heavily. The wind blew furiously. About midnight amid the howling of the wind, a knock was heard at the door. "Please, save me," a weak voice was heard crying. "Take me in."

Immediately the man was overcome with pity and began to cry for the poor fellow standing outside. As the minutes passed, the cries from outside continued, and the Jew inside continued to carry on about the poor fellow's condition. His wife finally asked him why he didn't let the fellow in the house. He answered, "If I let him in, then I wouldn't be able to have pity on him anymore."

(*)

🌷 🌷 🌷

A Jew once took a stranger home to eat for the Sabbath evening meal. On their way home the host noticed that a younger Jew was following them. He followed them home; he went into the house and even ate with them. After the meal was over, the host asked this guest if he knew the stranger. "Oh, yes," came the reply. "He's my son-in-law, and I've promised him support."

(*)

🌷 🌷 🌷

"Boy, did I get an order from Sears, Roebuck!" boasted Sam Fifnik to his competitor. "Two hundred thousand dollars!"

Moe looked at him, doubt all over his face. "Oh, yeah?"

"You don't believe me, huh?" shouted Fifnik. "Let me show you the cancellation."

🌼 🌼 🌼

Blattman, the lingerie king, turned to his chief salesman and said, gesturing to a beautiful young thing in the third row of the big new musical opening, "Man, I'd like to take her out again."

"You know her?" exclaimed his companion. "She looks like a show girl."

"No," said Blattman, "but I remember seeing her before, and I felt like taking her out that time, too."

🌼 🌼 🌼

"The food here is terrible," exclaimed Mrs. Feinberg as she pushed food into her mouth at the Royal Hooha Hotel in Miami Beach. "And not only that, but such small portions, too!"

🌼 🌼 🌼

Mrs. Bloomberg was complaining to her neighbor about the rats in her house. "I tried rat poison, but it doesn't work."

"Have you tried giving them rat biscuits?" asked her neighbor.

"If they don't like what we have in the kitchen," said Mrs. B., "then let them starve!"

♣ ♣ ♣

There was a very wealthy man in a small town. When he was dying, and the last doctor gave up, the heirs gave twenty kopecks to a number of poor people to say psalms so that the dying man might recover. One of the poor complained and said, "This man is so wealthy, he could give fifty kopecks per man or maybe even a whole ruble."

"Don't worry," said another. "With God's help they'll give out money again at the funeral."

(*)

♣ ♣ ♣

A country fellow came home from the city and told his wife, "Listen, love, did I see a fine young man in town. He's a gem. And I've decided to take him for a son-in-law. Tomorrow he is coming here, and we'll give him board for nothing."

His wife answered, "Have you lost your mind? Have you become senile lately? How can you take a son-in-law when you haven't got a daughter?"

"Who cares?" he answered. "Because of that, I should lose such a son-in-law?"

(*)

Lizabetta Steinberg was groaning in the twin bed next to Sam Steinberg's. "Oi, am I *thoisty*," she moaned. "Oi, am I thoisty."

After ten minutes of this, Sam finally woke up and staggered out of bed. "Gotta get up in two hours and go to work, and she wakes me up out of a sound sleep—" Nonetheless, he made his way to the kitchen and got Lizabetta a glass of cold water. Then he got back into bed, pulled his blanket over his head and somewhat disgruntled went back to sleep.

Five minutes later, Lizabetta started up again. "Oi, was I *thoisty*," she moaned. "Was I ever thoisty!"

❦ ❦ ❦

Harry Horowitz had a way with the women, and he never tired of exploiting his special gift. The only trouble was Lavonia Horowitz, Harry's wife, who grew more jealous with each passing year and with each of Harry's explanations, which were not only wearing thin but were becoming somewhat repetitious. One night Harry bedded down in the apartment of a young thing he had met in the garment showroom that afternoon, and he enjoyed himself more often and more deeply than was his wont. In short, he fell asleep and did not wake up until four in the morning. "Jumping Jehoshaphat!" Harry exclaimed and sat wretchedly on the side of the bed, racking his brain for something to say to Lavonia.

Suddenly his face brightened. He dialed a number and let it ring for a full two minutes. "Hello, Lavonia, darling," he said finally. "If those guys call you about the ransom, don't pay it. I just escaped and I'm on my way home."

❦ ❦ ❦

A marriage broker once came to a young man about a match. "I have a wonderful girl for you from a fine family. There's just one little problem, she has no money."

The young fellow responded, "I couldn't care less."

And just one more thing. "She doesn't hear too well out of one ear."

"I couldn't care less," he responded.

And another thing. "She doesn't see too well out of one eye."

He still just answered, "I couldn't care less."

"I must confess she limps a bit also."

"Oh, I couldn't care less."

"And furthermore, she has a slight hunch in her back."

"I couldn't care less."

The matchmaker just couldn't understand the young man's attitude. "What's going on here—nothing matters!"

The young man answered, "I couldn't care less because I'm not taking her anyway!"

(*)

❦ ❦ ❦

A family was sitting drinking tea calmly when a next-door neighbor broke into the house white as a sheet. He screamed, "Save my mother-in-law, she's hanging herself!"

There was a great confusion. Women began to faint, and children began to cry. Finally a young man called out, "Let's go before it's too late!"

He began running next door to see what was going on. As he ran, the neighbor grabbed him and said, "Don't rush, she's not dead yet!"

(*)

🌺 🌺 🌺

A yeshiva boy was once in the study hall of his yeshiva and saw a friend of his running up and down screaming, "*Oy vey*, good, *oy vey*, good."

He called to him, "Yankel, why are you carrying on like that? If everything is good, why were you screaming, *Oy vey?*"

Yankel, troubled, turned to him and said, "Listen, have I got an answer, it's beautiful, it's genius, but I've got one problem. I don't have a question."

(*)

🌺 🌺 🌺

It is told that Hershel Ostropolier once came to the local burial society and asked for money to buy grave clothes for his wife. His wife had died the day before.

They didn't say a word. A Jew has to bury his wife, and one must help him if possible.

A few hours later they arrived at Hershel's home with a casket. When they walked into the house, they saw Mrs. Ostropolier cooking.

"Hershel, what's going on? Why did you trick us like that?"

Hershel answered, "It shouldn't make any difference to you. If not today, tomorrow, but one of these days she'll be yours."

(*)

🌺 🌺 🌺

The bride is a lovely girl with money and from a wonderful family. There's just one little problem—she's just a little bit pregnant.

(*)

🌺 🌺 🌺

A small town decided to engage a preacher to speak weekly on Thursday afternoons for a period of two months. When the gentleman arrived in town on Wednesday afternoon, he was immediately escorted to the home of the richest man in town. After dinner, the preacher asked his host if he could borrow 100 rubles for a period of twenty-four hours. He would return the money right after the lecture. The host was very surprised by the request, but since the preacher was very respectable, he lent him the money. As he promised, the money was returned the following evening. This routine of borrowing 100 rubles and returning them shortly thereafter continued for five weeks. Finally the wealthy man asked why the preacher borrowed money and apparently did not use it. The preacher answered, "I really don't need the money, but when I have a hundred rubles in my pocket, I speak differently."

※ ※ ※

A Jew and his wife moved into a strange town. Unfortunately his wife became ill shortly thereafter. He needed a doctor, but he didn't know where to find one. He went out into the town and saw a fine-looking elderly gentleman. He tapped him on the shoulder and asked if he could suggest a doctor for his wife. "Of course," replied the gentleman, "you know we have many doctors, but the best one is Dr. Crinstein. He had the finest people in town for patients. Let me see, there was the late David Israel, Jake Rapaport, may he rest in peace, and the late Isaac Spektor—yes, indeed, he had the finest people in town for patients."

(*)

※ ※ ※

Every Thursday a certain not-too-clever peasant came into the town to sell cattle. One week a group of fellows got together and decided to trick him. One particular

Thursday, the peasant was leading a big fat ox. As he approached the town one of the group ran up to him and asked, "Ivan, how much do you want for that goat?" The peasant spit at him and went on.

Farther along he met another, who asked him the same question. "How much do you want for your goat?"

At that point Ivan got all mixed up. This same stunt was repeated five or six times in succession, and soon Ivan himself believed that he was leading a goat and sold the animal at that price.

(*)

🌺 🌺 🌺

Once the teacher in public school asked a Jewish student the following question: "I borrowed a hundred rubles from your father, and I've paid him back fifty. How much do I owe him?"

The boy thought and asked, "You borrowed money from my father?"

The teacher got angry and said, "Fool, what's the difference? I didn't borrow money from him. But *if* I borrowed one hundred and paid back fifty, how much do I still owe?"

The child answered, "One hundred rubles."

The teacher became furious and said, "Numskull, you don't know any arithmetic."

"No," said the student, "I know arithmetic, but you don't know my father!"

(*)

🌺 🌺 🌺

A Jew once went to find out how to use a telephone. He had to speak with someone. As it was, he didn't know what to do. He asked the girl sitting at the desk in the telephone office for instructions. "With one hand you hold the receiver and with the other you dial."

The Jew looked back at her and said, "That's fine, but with which hand do I talk?"

(*)

🌷 🌷 🌷

A Jew once wanted to buy a cow. He went into town, but he couldn't find any, so he bought a bull instead. Soon there was a plague in the town that he lived in, and all the cows died. The bull that he purchased also died. The Jew went over to the dead bull and said, "*Oy*, you bull, you, when it came to milking, you were a bull, but when it comes to dying, you're a cow!"

(*)

🌷 🌷 🌷

Mrs. Feinberg had just checked into the Hilton Hotel in Manhattan and was highly indignant. She rang the manager's office and almost screamed into the receiver: "What kind of place is this you're running? I'm a decent middle-aged lady, and across the airshaft is a man standing naked in front of an open window! And he's a *goy*, at that!"

The manager tried his best to calm the furious lady and assured her that he would be right up to smooth things over. When he arrived in Mrs. Feinberg's room, he made immediately for the window that gave on the airshaft and peered out. "But, lady, there's no one across the airshaft! All I can see is darkened windows!"

Mrs. Feinberg looked down at him with an air of disdain. "Idiot!" she said. "He's four floors below this one. Come stand up here on the bureau with me, and you'll see the man I'm talking about!"

🌺 🌺 🌺

The late Ben Bernie once related this episode about his mother's seventieth birthday. As a present, he gave her a magnum of champagne and a large tin of imported caviar. He telephoned her on the following day to inquire if she was pleased with her birthday gifts.

"Benny, I'm not complaining, believe me," she said. "The ginger ale was fine, but frankly the huckleberries tasted from herring!"

🌺 🌺 🌺

Mama checked into a hotel, and the desk clerk called out, "Page boy!" The boy appeared at once and carried her luggage upstairs to her room.

Later, after a shopping tour, Mama returned to the

hotel with several bulky packages. She went to the desk clerk and asked: "Mister, would you be so kind to call again the page *goy?*"

🌷 🌷 🌷

SON: Dad, what was your ambition when you were a little boy?
FATHER: To wear long pants. I got my wish, too. There isn't another man in America who wears his pants longer than I do.

🌷 🌷 🌷

From the Budapest of the old days comes the tale of the beggar Wentzel who visited the home of the enormously wealthy widow Kaposvar and begged the servant to usher him into madame's presence. His wish granted, Wentzel immediately fell to his knees and began to weep. "For five days, Madame Kaposvar, my wife and I have had nothing to eat but an old crust of bread. My children are literally starving to death before my eyes. And the landlord plans to evict us tomorrow morning unless I can raise a bit of money." Wentzel paused, and out of the corner of his eye he could see that the rich widow was beginning to be moved by his recital of woe. "My loving wife," he went on, "is ill, and we can't afford medicine. She will die of the fever unless I can get some assistance." Now

Wentzel observed tears standing in the widow's eyes. "Not only that," he continued, "but Pesach is upon us, and I haven't a drop of wine or a piece of matzoh to celebrate the holiday in the proper spirit."

Now the old widow Kaposvar was weeping unashamedly and wringing her hands. She pulled the bell rope, and the butler appeared immediately. "Throw this man out," screamed the old dowager. "He's breaking my heart!"

❉ ❉ ❉

Tevye, the dairyman, one of the best figures of Sholom Aleichem, once remarked, "With God's help I starved to death."

Ill luck is here attributed to the disfavor of God, but the *shlemiel* knows somewhere that he himself stands behind the wings as the stage manager of his own identity. Many Jewish proverbs accentuate the purposefulness of bad luck as if they recognized that the *shlemiel* is prone to misfortune. Here are a few instances: "When a *shlemiel* kills a chicken, it walks; when he winds a clock, it stops," or "He falls on his back and breaks his nose."

The *shlemiel* is thus a certain type, easily defined or characterized psychologically, a type met with not only among Jews, but also among Gentiles. The *shlemiel* is the hidden architect of his misfortune. The ironic phrase "Jewish luck" hints at a more general connotation beyond the narrow limitations of an ineffectual Jewish type.

71

"When you are six, you believe the penis is there only to urinate. When you are sixty, you know it." Another observation has the same character: "When you get old, you forget to close your fly, and when you get still older, you forget to open it."

(*Leo Rosten*)

❀ ❀ ❀

The difference between the *shlemiel* and the *shlimazl* is accentuated in the business world. When a *shlemiel* receives a check for $100, he loses it. When that luckless fellow known as a *shlimazl* receives a check for $100, the only one who can cash it is the man to whom he owes $99.

❀ ❀ ❀

For two decades Grossman, the bagel man, was a familiar sight on Orchard Street. All day long, year in and year out, he called, "Bagels, fresh bagels—below cost!" Whenever he made a sale, he would dip into his basket, hand the customer the bagels, and mutter piteously, "I'm losing money."

One day a stranger approached. "Look, if you are losing money with every sale, why don't you quit?"

"Quit?" echoed Grossman, peering at the man as though he were insane. "Then tell me, how will I make a living?"

❦ ❦ ❦

The late Polly Adler, author of *A House Is Not a Home,* once contemplated using this sign in her "establishment": IT'S A BUSINESS DOING PLEASURE WITH YOU

❦ ❦ ❦

A merchant, notorious as a poor payer, was arguing with his wholesaler over the price of a bolt of cloth. For a half hour they haggled and scolded until only a penny separated them.

"Let me ask you a question," said the exasperated wholesaler. "We're old friends, and I know you well enough to realize I'll have a long wait for my money. In fact, I might not get paid at all. So why do you haggle like this, especially for a measly cent?"

"Because I like you," said the merchant. "The lower I can get the cost, the less you'll lose when I don't pay."

❦ ❦ ❦

The youth was telling his fiancée about his family background. "Papa lost everything in the twenty-nine Wall Street crash."

73

"You mean he was a big banker?" the girl asked, surprised.

"No, not that. A ruined financier jumped out of the thirty-fifth-story window of the Securities Building and landed on Papa's pushcart."

❦ ❦ ❦

SON: POP, why can't we have wall-to-wall carpets like other people?
FATHER: Listen, when I was your age, we were lucky to have wall-to-wall floors!

❦ ❦ ❦

Phil Fine, owner of Fine's Fashionable Footwear, a store on LaSalle in Chicago's Loop, was a notoriously poor payer. There was scarcely a manufacturer or jobber to whom he did not owe money. It wasn't that business was bad—the man just hated to pay his bills.

One morning he telephoned Schneider, one of his suppliers, and asked for another consignment of merchandise.

"You already owe me for three months," Schneider protested.

"I'll pay up the whole bill next month," Fine solemnly promised.

"W-e-l-l, just this one more time."

"You won't regret it. Thanks."

"To tell you the truth, Mr. Fine, I wish I had a hundred customers like you. I'd be much better off."

"Now you're making fun of me," said Fine. "You know I'm a slow payer."

"No, I'm not making fun of you at all. I really would be better off with a hundred customers like you. The trouble is, I have *two* hundred."

🌷 🌷 🌷

Old-timers swear that this is a true anecdote.

An eager young man solicited the advice of the late Bernard Baruch at the turn of the century. Although a young man himself, Baruch had already become a financial tycoon.

"Tell me, is there any sure and certain way to make a million dollars?" asked the youth.

"Yes, one," replied Baruch. "All you need do is buy a million bags of flour at a dollar a bag and then sell them for two dollars each."

🌷 🌷 🌷

Two Jewish mendicants once went to see Baron Rothschild. One said to the other, "You know what, you came first, and I'll wait for you." He went inside, and a secretary asked him what he wanted. He said that he wanted some money. He was then sent to a second secretary and then to a teller. The teller heard him out, gave him a note, and sent him to a third secretary. This secretary read the note, wrote another, and sent him to the head secretary. This process continued for nearly an hour, and finally, he arrived at the desk of the last secretary, who told him to leave the premises immediately if not sooner. When he got outside, his companion asked him if he had gotten anything. "No," he replied, "but a system like Rothschild's I've never seen."

(*)

🌷 🌷 🌷

A Jew once went into a clothing store to buy a coat. He looked at a few coats and said to the owner, "Listen, I can't stand bargaining, and it's my nature to pay what I'm asked. Please tell me the final price."

"You didn't even have to tell me," said the owner. "I only have one price."

The Jew asked, "How much is this coat?"

"What should I tell you; I won't tell you thirty rubles, twenty-five rubles or twenty rubles. However, I cannot take less than eighteen."

The Jew responded, "And I won't tell you three rubles or four or five, but I'm not giving you more than ten."

The owner said to a clerk, "Pack up that coat!"

(*)

🌷 🌷 🌷

A Jew was once robbed. He called the police, and when they came, they saw that the thief had only taken small things from the room. In the same room were small diamond-studded figurines, other gold and silver articles, but these the thief didn't touch. A few days later, the thief was found, and he was also a Jew. They took him to court, and the judge asked him to explain the strange crime. "Please," said the thief, "don't ask me that. My wife has bugged me about that much too much already."

(*)

🌷 🌷 🌷

Once a thief entered a garden, stole a basket of carrots, and put them in a sack. The owner of the garden caught him and stopped him. "Why are you stealing my carrots?"

"Don't blame me," he said. "I didn't want to steal them. There was a rain and wind storm, so I came into the garden to lie down under a tree. The wind blew, so I grabbed at the grass for an anchor, and I pulled out a carrot. I did this again and again, and every time I pulled up a carrot."

The owner asked him, "That's fine, but how did they get into your sack?"

He replied, "You know, I've asked myself that same question!"

(*)

🌷 🌷 🌷

Once in a small town lived a winemaker. That means it was his business to make wine. There was plenty of water in the town; but this winemaker held that a lot of wine was not healthy, and he was afraid that the non-Jews and Hasidim that drank his wine would become drunk. He had a wonderful business; he was also a pious Jew and gave a lot to charity. However, life must end, and when he was dying, he called his sons to the bedside and told them, "I'm dying, but I know you'll carry on my business, so I must tell you a very important secret in the winemaking business that you should know. That wine can also be made from grapes."

(*)

🌻 🌻 🌻

If my diet had not been so successful, I might have been in much better shape today. A few years ago my doctor gave me a diet which I followed religiously. At the end of two months I had lost twenty-one pounds, and I felt better than ever. Because of the great success of this diet, I said to myself: "If that is all there is to this, I can do it any time, so why not wait for a more appropriate moment?"

And that's where it stands now.

The Yiddishe Mama

FROM Vietnam comes the story of a religious service held in a makeshift chapel erected just behind the front lines. It was Christmas Eve, and the Catholic chaplain had managed somehow to borrow a squeaky foot-pedal organ from a nearby village. As it turned out, however, no one in the combat platoon could play the instrument except Moscowitz, who had had one month of organ lessons soon after his thirteenth birthday back in Brooklyn. Would he play for the men? the chaplain wanted to know. He would, said Moscowitz, but he was embarrassed to confess that he had mastered only one song. The title? "A Yiddishe Mama." After the brief recital Moscowitz bowed very formally, and the men broke up in laughter. The chaplain, nothing daunted, turned the occasion into a mini-sermon about brotherhood. "Don't forget," he told them, "the mother of our Lord was also a Yiddishe mama."

🌸 🌸 🌸

Gertrude, queen of the Danes in Shakespeare's melancholy tragedy, was probably Jewish. The giveaway is in the scene known to scholars of the drama as "the bedroom interview." In this confrontation the young Hamlet scolds his mother for her infidelity to the memory of his father, the deceased king. He curses her for her bad taste in marrying Claudius. He berates her for her middle-aged lechery. For a moment, he seems to be on the brink of either spitting on the floor in disgust or belting the old lady across the chops. Just then the ghost reappears to Hamlet and tells him to lay off: "Leave her to heaven," says the old man—and to the pangs of her own conscience. Gertrude's reaction to all this? She's worried about the *boychik.* "What's the matter, darling?" she asks him, when she realizes that he's been holding a conversation with the air. If she doesn't actually get up and make him some chicken soup, it's only because the royal kitchen is closed up for the night.

ר״ש

🌼 🌼 🌼

A folktale made the rounds of the Lower East Side some fifty years ago that illustrated the same Yiddishe Mama principle. A beggar came to the back door of Rosie Greenblatt's home and pleaded for a little something to eat. Rosie, nothing loath, cooked him an overwhelming supper and set it steaming on the kitchen table. The hungry fellow made short work of this feast, but as he was mopping up, he managed to slip one of Rosie's sterling silver spoons into the side pocket of his raggedy coat. And out the door he went, without so much as a thank-you for poor Rosie.

But she had observed him out of the corner of one eye, and she flew out the back door in pursuit, screaming, "Wait! Stop! I've got to tell you something! That spoon is *milchik* [that is, under Jewish dietary law, reserved for dairy products, not to be used for meat]!"

🌷 🌷 🌷

Overconcern also pops up in other sorts of inappropriate situations. Kirk Douglas is fond of telling about the day he called his mother to tell her he had just signed a fantastic contract with a big Hollywood studio. "It guarantees me a million dollars, Ma," Douglas exclaimed.

"Never mind about that," she told him. "You looked skinny in your last movie. Are you getting enough to eat?"

🌷 🌷 🌷

Then there's my cousin Melvin, who lives in upstate New York and still remembers the day when as a boy of ten or eleven he heard an announcement on the radio about an impending solar eclipse. Rushing into the kitchen where his mother was preparing supper, Melvin asked breathlessly, "Mama, can I go out and watch the eclipse?"

"Yes," said his mama, "but be careful not to get too close."

🌷 🌷 🌷

Mrs. Gittelson was beaming with pride. A newcomer to America, she had worked in a neighborhood dress shop and had just received her first week's salary. It came in the form of a check, which was a novelty to Mrs. Gittelson. She took the word of the other girls in the shop and went to the Chemical Bank to cash it. "You'll have to endorse this, ma'am," said the teller.

"What means endorse?" inquired the lady.

"Sign it on the back," explained the teller, "just the same as you do when closing a letter."

Mrs. Gittelson giggled and blushed, but you could tell she was happy nonetheless. She took the pen he offered her and wrote on the back of the check: "Lovingly yours, Miriam Gittelson."

🌷 🌷 🌷

Old man Baumgarten was depressed. Once again, after thirty-two years of marriage, he had forgotten his wife's birthday. Contrite, he rushed home and took her by the hands. Looking deep into her faded eyes, Papa Baumgarten said, "Sadie, I will make it all up to you. Tell me, and forgive me my absentmindedness, what is your favorite flower?"

84

"As if you didn't know, Papa, after all these years! It's Pillsbury, of course!"

🌸 🌸 🌸

Dr. Ospenok took off his spectacles and stared at the floor. Finally he looked up. "All right, Mrs. Gross, the examination is over. I believe in being honest with my patients, and I must inform you that as we grow older, our bodies begin to decline. We can't fight off infection the way we used to. We don't heal as rapidly. And then, to make matters worse, we are subject to all sorts of ailments after we reach a certain age. I'm sorry, Mrs. Gross"—he shook his head—"but we doctors cannot perform miracles. You can't expect me to make you younger."

"So who's asking to be made younger?" replied Mrs. Gross indignantly. "What I want is to grow older!"

🌸 🌸 🌸

Phyllis called her mother from college and breathed heavily with excitement into the telephone. "Guess what, Mama? I'm calling from Morton's apartment to tell you the news. Prepare yourself! Morton and I are engaged!"

"I know, Phyllis, that's what worries me. What are you engaged in?"

🌸 🌸 🌸

Jewish one-upmanship is also related to the art of survival and sometimes takes the form: just because you win doesn't mean I lose.

❦ ❦ ❦

When Chaim Weizmann was President of Israel, a member of his Cabinet entered his office one morning and discovered him in the act of shining his shoes. "Mr. President," exclaimed the astonished official, "shining your own shoes!"

Weizmann kept right on polishing with the rag and asked, "Maybe you expected to find me shining someone else's shoes?"

❦ ❦ ❦

Former heavyweight champion Buddy Baer performed in the movie *Quo Vadis,* in which Hollywood spectacular he pits his strength against an enraged bull who is trying to get at Deborah Kerr in the Colosseum. After a few moments of dramatic struggle Baer twists and wrestles and succeeds in breaking the bull's neck. The day following this incredible exploit Buddy received a beautiful chunk of raw steak in his dressing room with a note which read: "From the manager: this is from the bull you killed." Buddy sent it back with his own note attached: "To the manager: I refuse to eat a fellow actor."

The Yiddishe Mama

🌷 🌷 🌷

Sally and David Cohn were young, attractive, affluent, and happily married. Everyone believed they were among that rare class of mortals who seem blessed by fortune, destined to live out their lives without trouble or worry. The Ladies' Auxiliary was therefore doubly shaken up to see David having lunch at Longchamps with a stunning blonde, whom he treated with obvious intimacy and affection. Bad luck for Sally, for she was with the tea-drinking ladies and she saw as clearly as anyone what was going on. When she got home, Sally Cohn cried a little, and that night she told David that she knew. "Look," he said. "Why upset yourself? The girl is my mistress, but you are my beloved wife. I love you more than ever, and I don't want us ever to break up. If you'll bear with me until the affair runs its course, I'll promise never to stray again. And just to show how wonderful I think you are, I'm buying you a new outfit tomorrow afternoon at Saks, and then we're going out to dinner and the theater."

What could Sally say? Struggling through a few bad moments, by the following day she was reconciled to the arrangement. That evening as she and David sat chatting and dining in the Four Seasons, they suddenly spotted Marty Greenspan, one of the executives in David's office. Marty was having dinner with a beautiful redhead. "Look," Sally whispered, nudging her husband, "there's Marty Greenspan. Who's that girl he's with?"

David leaned forward and murmured, "That's *his* mistress."

Sally gave Marty's companion a long, slow, careful inspection and then turned to her husband. Clasping her pretty little hands together with delight, she exclaimed: "You know something? I like ours much better!"

🕎 🕎 🕎

Harry Horowitz, he of the suspicious wife, was still philandering and still thinking up ways to get around Lavonia's nagging. Finally, one night at a poker game in desperation Harry put up his wife as stakes—against the other fellow's yacht. Harry lost. The next morning Harry announced as diplomatically as possible the result of the previous night's wager. "You lost me in a poker game!" exclaimed Lavonia. "How could you do such a thing?"

Harry explained as calmly as he could that it was no easy task. "Me with a royal flush," he said ruefully, "and I had to fold!"

🕎 🕎 🕎

Max Bubbleham, the famous Jewish Civil War general and Southern philanthropist, once checked into the Tafeta Hotel in Montgomery, Alabama, and left strict instructions to be called at six thirty the next morning. The desk clerk and the bell captain both assured him that he would be called, sho'nuff, at the appointed hour. Bright and early the next morning Bubbleham was roused. He shaved, donned his white linen suit, and strode out into the lobby. "Mawning, Cuhnel Whitefish," drawled the clean-up girl. Bubbleham was annoyed at the misidentification, but he walked toward the dining room without replying. "Well, good mornin', Colonel Whitefish," said the maître d'. "I trust you slept well."

Now Bubbleham began to feel a bit ruffled. But when he had taken a seat at the breakfast table and another of the guests had greeted him with great familiarity as Colonel Whitefish, Bubbleham began to feel an unbearable sort of misgiving. He turned pale, excused himself, and rushed to the men's room at the back of the lobby. Once inside, he made straight for the mirror and looked unflinchingly at his reflection. "By God!" he exclaimed. "Just as I thought! They woke up the wrong man!"

🌺 🌺 🌺

Eustacia Gugenblatt was a shy old lady who loved pickled herring. Once the craving was upon her, she could not resist leaving her snug apartment to brave the muggers, mashers, kidnappers, and con men—all this for a meal of pickled herring. One night Eustacia Gugenblatt betook herself with a ravenous appetite to Gluckstern's Restaurant, there to savor the specialty of the house. When the waiter set the plate before her, with three magnificent silvery pickled herring waiting to be attacked, Eustacia was ecstatic. She dug her fork into the nearest specimen and was about to slice off a piece with her knife, when the herring looked up at her and said:

"Ouch! That hurts! How would you like someone jabbing you with a fork?" Eustacia was both mortified and terrified. She dropped the knife and fork, screamed a little old lady's scream, and fled from the place.

Months passed.

Then one night the craving returned, and Eustacia decided to try again. After all, it was probably her imagination about the talking fish. And so she sat once more at Gluckstern's, and again a plate of choice herring was placed before her, and this time Eustacia closed her eyes, stuck her fork into the herring, and was in the act of slicing off a delicious morsel when she heard the voice again: "Hey, lady! That hurts! Watch the way you stick me in the midsection!" Once again Eustacia panicked and fled the scene in a state of awful emotion.

A year went by before it hit her again.

This time, as she adjusted her hat in front of the mirror, she smiled slyly and traveled uptown to the seafood emporium operated by Barney Greengrass. As she dug her fork into the side of the beautiful pickled herring before her, the creature raised his head in some surprise. "What's the matter, lady?" it asked. "You don't eat at Gluckstern's any more?"

🌺 🌺 🌺

A weary bartender decided to take a vacation and get away from the rush and bustle of the big city. He found himself a little itty-bitty town on a map of New Jersey, packed a bag, and hopped a bus. Settled down for a ten-day stay at a rural inn, the bartender decided to unwind by taking a walk through a bona fide country field. On his way through the high grass, he found himself face to face with a grasshopper, who happened (though the bartender did not know it) to be Jewish. "Hey, grasshopper!" the bartender exclaimed. "Do you know you're famous?"

The grasshopper smiled and performed the grasshopper equivalent of a cat's purr.

"Absolutely," the bartender went on. "Back in the big city there's a very popular drink named after you."

The grasshopper was both pleased and surprised. "You mean they got a cocktail named Irving?" he croaked.

❋ ❋ ❋

A Jewish woman comes home in tears from seeing the doctor. "He told me I got tuberculosis and must die yet," she wails.

"What, a big, fat woman like you?" says her husband. "That's ridiculous."

He rushes to the doctor's office and begins berating him.

"Now just a minute," says the doctor, "I didn't tell your wife she had tuberculosis; I told her she has too big a *tochus* and must go on a diet."

❋ ❋ ❋

A professor of zoology at Harvard, some years ago, asked his graduate students, among whom were several foreigners, to write papers on the elephant.

91

A German student wrote: "An Introduction to the Bibliography for the Study of the Elephant."

A French student wrote: "The Love Life of the Elephant."

An English student wrote: "Elephant Hunting."

A Canadian student wrote: "Breeding Bigger and Better Elephants."

Izzy Kaplan, also a student in the class, wrote: "The Elephant and the Jewish Problem."

❦ ❦ ❦

"Irving," scolded the small boy's mother, "your face is clean, but how did you manage to get your hands so dirty?"

"Washing my face," replied Irving.

❦ ❦ ❦

"What would you like for Chanukah?" the mother asked her ten-year-old daughter.

"A mirror, Mommy."

"What a peculiar request! Why?"

"Because," sighed the girl, "I'm getting too big to make up in the doorknob."

❦ ❦ ❦

The Yiddishe Mama

Lennie Lichtenstein met Sarah Saperstein at a dance, and it was love at first sight. "Don't do it, Lennie," warned his friends. "She's a nag, and you'll be henpecked for the rest of your life." Lennie laughed at such discouragement. What did he care! He was going to make the beautiful Sarah his own! And besides, it was all untrue. Those guys down at the soda shop were jealous; that was all. On his wedding day Lennie was so happy his heart was singing. After the dinner party, he and Sarah took a cab uptown to the bridal suite in the Manhattan Towers. They kissed all the way up in the elevator and all the way down the corridor. When they got to the door of the suite, Lennie tenderly lifted his bride and started to enter. "Wipe your feet, you big *shlemiel!*" Sarah reminded him.

❧ ❧ ❧

The Vietnam War was raging on all sides of the small group of American soldiers. The sergeant drew up his isolated squad and barked: "This is it, men! The time has come to charge the Vietcong. Get your bayonets ready— it's now man against man in hand-to-hand combat!"

Private Albert Silverstein raised his hand.

"Yeah, Silverstein," snapped the noncom. "What is it?"

"Sarge," quavered the private. "It's man against man?"

"You heard me!"

"Look," said Silverstein desperately, "how about showing me my man? Maybe he and I can work this thing out by ourselves!"

A devout young Jew left his little village in Russia to seek his fortune in America. Many years later, having amassed his share of earthly goods, he decided to visit his aged parents in the land of his birth and to relive a few nostalgic moments of his boyhood.

His eighty-year-old mother scarcely recognized him, so much had he changed.

"Your clothes are so strange!" she murmured. "But why aren't you wearing a beard like a good Jew?"

"But, Mama, all men shave in the United States."

"And the food? You at least keep a kosher kitchen in your house?"

"Well, to tell the truth, Mama, it is almost impossible to observe our dietary laws."

The old lady wiped a tear from her eye with a corner of her apron. Then a sudden, fearful thought struck her.

"Tell me, are you still circumcised?"

❧ ❧ ❧

The biggest anti-Semite in the Ukraine around the turn of the century was a mounted officer named Torom the Terrible, who punished and abused the Jews in his district every time he had a few drinks. When Torom's reputation was at its height, he got drunk one night and went strutting around the village, throwing rocks through Jewish shopwindows and barging into the homes of Jewish families, breaking furniture and scream-

94

ing insults. In one modest house Torom found an attractive young lady holding a little baby.

"What is your name?" he demanded.

"Olga Fishbein," the girl replied, completely unintimidated.

"And what is the name of that miserable child there?" screamed the officer, gesturing at Olga's baby.

Unflinching she stared him in the eyes and replied, "The baby's name is Torom."

This struck Torom as amusing. "Ha-ha-ha," he barked. "You and your husband must be very stupid or very cowardly to give your child that name. Do you not know that I am the worst enemy of your people in this region?"

Olga Fishbein smiled indulgently and replied, "I know very well what you are. And I have no husband. You see, I have had many lovers, and the baby was born out of wedlock."

🌷 🌷 🌷

An imaginative member of a Chicago finance company sent the following letter to one of his delinquent accounts:

DEAR MR. LEVY:

After checking our records, we note that we have done more for you than your own mother did. We carried you for fifteen months.

🌷 🌷 🌷

Mama, Papa, and little Isidor were at the supper table.

"Papa," asked Isidor, "What's the difference between a husband and a bachelor?"

Papa winked at Mama, and in a solemn voice he answered his son, "A bachelor, Isidor, is a man who comes to work every morning from a different direction."

☙ ☙ ☙

It is sometimes impossible to predict the reaction of a doting Jewish mother. Here is a case in point:

When Oscar Levant, the famed piano virtuoso and entertainer, telephoned his mother and informed her that he had proposed to his sweetheart and she had accepted, his mother answered, "All right, Oscar; good! I'm glad to hear it. But did you practice your piano today?"

☙ ☙ ☙

The rescue party was small and select. The forestry service had rounded up two hunters, a med student, and a priest. As they approached the disaster area, littered with still-smoldering fragments of the airplane, they could make out a few survivors stumbling absently about. One of these was an old gent wearing a yarmulke. He was muttering to himself and making the sign of the cross, over and over. The priest went immediately into action. He strode forward and put his arms around the shoulder of the aged Jewish gentleman. "Welcome to our church, old fellow," he said to the dazed survivor. "I am gratified, deeply gratified, to see that your narrow brush with death has turned you in the direction of the true faith."

The old guy stopped muttering, stopped stumbling around, and stopped crossing himself. He looked at the smiling clergyman and said, "What in hell are you talking about, the church, the true faith?"

The priest spluttered a bit and said, "Why, you, old-timer, you're so glad to be alive that you're making the sign of the cross. Are you not aware of its significance?"

The old guy grunted and laughed. "Sign of the cross, phooey! I am just checking to see if everything is intact in its proper place. When you saw my hand moving from my forehead to my abdomen and from one shoulder to the other, I was satisfying myself as to the condition of my spectacles, my testicles, my wallet, my cigars."

💮 💮 💮

The transit companies in various cities issue a weekly pass or commutation ticket which, for two or three dollars, permits the holder to ride the buses all week without extra payment of fares.

Comedian Alan King tells of the time his family lived next door to the McCarthy family. One day, his mother, Minnie, borrowed her neighbor Mary's commutation ticket.

"When that Prussian-background man in uniform, the conductor, looked at Minnie and saw the name 'Mary

McCarthy' on the passbook, he demanded that Mama sign her name on open-blank RR ticket," Alan King said.

"Mama looked at him and huffed: 'I'm sorry, General, but on Saturday I never write!' "

🌼 🌼 🌼

The best advertiser is a Jewish mother. Take the case of the Yiddishe Mama and her grown son who went to Coney Island. The son, who was a physician and should have known better, went swimming too soon after eating and almost at once was in distress. The mother saw him struggling in the water. Frantically she ran along the beach, shrieking at the top of her voice: "Help! Somebody, please help! My son, the Park Avenue doctor, he's drowning!"

🌼 🌼 🌼

A Jew returned from Germany to his little town. When he spoke to the rabbi about his trip, he was asked what was new in the outside world. "I have heard," said the rabbi, "that there are great miracles going on there, that no one has told me about."

"I can give you a few examples," came the reply. "They have trolley cars—they are wagons that go without horses and use electricity instead. You don't have to walk anymore. You just hop on the trolley, and it takes you wherever they want to go. There are also trains. You can travel from Kovno to Vilna in thirty minutes. And there are telegraph offices and telephones. You can communicate quickly, almost immediately, with people far away. And," he said, "there are many, many more things."

The rabbi answered the Jew by telling him that truly these inventions were miraculous. But the rabbi had one question still. "What's their hurry?"

🌷 🌷 🌷

Seymour Epstein was a window decorator at a chic Fifth Avenue ladies' wear shop, and in his spare time he was studying ballet at the studio of a dear friend on Avenue C. One cloudy afternoon Seymour took the crosstown bus to go to his ballet lesson, and when he got off the bus, he forgot his umbrella. The bus driver looked back and saw the pearl-handled object hooked around the metal bar on the back of one of the seats. "Hey, *fruit!*" he called to Seymour, who was mincing toward the corner. Seymour looked back. "You forgot your fairy *wand!*" called the bus driver.

Seymour returned to the front of the bus and, blushing furiously, walked down the aisle to pick up the umbrella. As he dismounted, he turned to the driver, pointed the tip of the umbrella directly at his face, and said, "Magic wand, magic wand, turn that man to *dreck!*"

🌷 🌷 🌷

Mrs. Harold Dresser of Los Angeles writes to tell me of the morning she heard the tin whistle of the bakery truck making its suburban rounds. The deliveries were made by a Mexican-American driver who counted change only in Spanish and often had trouble managing the English language.

This morning he slowed in front of the Dresser house and Mrs. Dresser called to him, "One egg bread, please."

He simply looked at her.

"One egg bread, please," said Mrs. Dresser loudly, going on the assumption that if she made her request more noisily, he would understand more easily.

"One what?" asked the driver.

"Egg bread!" screamed Mrs. Dresser.

"Oh," said the Mexican. "You mean a *challah*."

🌱 🌱 🌱

At the bridge club one day the ladies were comparing notes about their gynecologists. Mina Hossenpfeffer was singing the praises of a doctor she had visited for the first time the previous week. "That Dr. Gladfehlder!" she cooed. "Soch a gentleman! Soch an eggspert! He makes me feel understood inside and out! I love him!"

Minnie Goldspritz turned pale. A year earlier she had been examined by Dr. Gladfehlder to see why she and Sam could not make a baby. The doctor had given her extensive tests and then had reported that she had an uncorrectable condition: a fission in the passage. "My dear," he had told her sympathetically, "if you conceive, it will be a miracle." Now Minnie was fuming at the very memory. Tears came to her eyes when she thought of the awful thing he had told her. "I don't trust him an inch!" she said with a touch of hysteria, taking out trump. "He told me—why, it was ridiculous! He told me I had a fish in my passage, and if I ever had a baby, it would be a mackerel!"

🌷 🌷 🌷

A guest was sitting at the table waiting to be served. Noodle soup was brought to the table. The host began to eat. The soup was very hot, and the host burned his tongue. He actually began to cry. The guest asked him why he was crying. He was ashamed to tell the truth, so he said that he was crying because his father had recently passed away. The host really hoped that the guest would also burn his tongue. The guest took a spoonful of soup and also burned himself severely. He too cried. The host asked him why he was crying. "I'm crying," he said, "because your father didn't die ten years ago."

🌷 🌷 🌷

A fellow invited two fellow Jews to tea. They both came and were discussing the fine points of Jewish law when the wife of the host brought out the tea and two little cakes. As it was, one cake was smaller than the other. Each guest asked the other to take the larger cake, and each refused. Finally, Isaac took the larger when immediately Jacob spoke up. "Where are your manners?" he asked. "If I had chosen first, I would have taken the smaller one."

"Really," responded Isaac. "If that's the case, everything is all right, because the smaller one is sitting here waiting for you."

(*)

🕎 🕎 🕎

Sidney Fedderman, called Reb Sidney, was on his deathbed. Around the aged and highly respected patriarch had gathered members of the family. His wife, Rachel, stood toward the head of the bed holding the old man's hand. "Rachel," breathed the venerable grandfather, "is Nathan here?" Nathan was the oldest son.

"Yes, Papa," she assured him. "Nathan is here. He came last night and hasn't left your side for eighteen hours."

The old man sighed. "Is Benjamin here?" Benjamin was the number two son.

"Yes, Papa," his wife replied. "Benjamin is here and has been weeping all afternoon."

Reb Sidney closed his eyes. "Is Gershon here?" he whispered. Gershon was the son-in-law.

"Yes, Papa, Gershon was the first to arrive, and he's standing at the foot of the bed."

The old man folded his hands and said, "Come close, Mama, I want to tell you something."

Mrs. Fedderman leaned down close to the old man's

face. "If Nathan is here, and Benjamin is here"—and now the Reb's voice grew loud and angry—"and Gershon is here, THEN WHO THE HELL IS MINDING THE STORE?"

🌷 🌷 🌷

The mourners filed past the coffin, some sobbing, some sighing, and Mrs. Mittelman murmured, "Look at him. How peaceful he looks . . . how relaxed . . . so tan . . . so healthy!"

"Why not?" replied Mittelman. "He just spent three weeks in Miami."

🌷 🌷 🌷

A Jewish patient, swears David Geller, told his psychiartist: "I dreamed last night I saw my mother in the kitchen, but when she turned around, she had your face. This disturbed me so much it woke me and I couldn't sleep anymore. This morning, when I finally got out of bed, I drank a Coke and came right to you. Doctor, can you tell me why I had that dream?"

Answered the psychiatrist: "A Coke? That's a breakfast?"

🌷 🌷 🌷

"Mrs. Yifnik," said the psychiatrist, "there is nothing physically wrong with your little boy. But I must tell you this: He has an Oedipus complex."

"Oedipus-shmedipus!" snorted Mrs. Yifnik. "Just so long as he loves his mother!"

🌼 🌼 🌼

Dr. Max Mandelstamm was the greatest Russian eye specialist of his day, and the faculty of the University of Kiev proposed his appointment to a full professorship. The senate of the university, however, could not agree to this appointment because the candidate was a Jew. When Dr. Mandelstamm heard of what had transpired at the meeting of the senate, he hurriedly penned the following note to the president, and asked his furnace tender to deliver it:

"I respectfully recommend the bearer of this letter to the Chair of Ophthalmology at the University. He is not an eye specialist, but he answers to your requirements. He is a Christian and has for years been my dependable janitor."

🌼 🌼 🌼

A young bachelor, a sort of mama's boy, overly protected by his mother, came home one night a little under the weather, which was unusual. His clothes were rumpled, and he fell sound asleep. His mother wanted to get his suit pressed, and she emptied his pockets, and out fell a lipstick. With trembling hands she picked up the lipstick, deeply chagrined, disappointed and sad, and she looked at it and saw the inscription. "Helena Rubinstein," said Mama. "Well, thank God, at least she's a Jewish girl."

(*)

☙ ☙ ☙

Children. But how little does "children" convey that bursting sentiment *naches* and the pride with which Jews say *kinder*.

Sometimes this parental feeling is carried to startling extremes. My wife remembers a neighbor who was so fierce in her maternal affections that when her *nogoodnik* son was arrested, for some petty infraction of the law, she returned from visiting him in jail to announce, "You never *saw* such a beautiful jail as my Morris is in!"

☙ ☙ ☙

Little Benny was watching his mother bake cookies. He stood there for a long time, then said, "Mama, why don't you ask me something?"

"What should I ask you, *in mitn drinnen?*"

"You could ask me, 'You want a cookie, Benny?' "

☙ ☙ ☙

Two klutzes were discussing their wives. "My wife drives me crazy; every night she dreams she married a millionaire!"

"That drives you crazy? You're lucky. *My* wife dreams she's married to a millionaire in the daytime."

(Leo Rosten)

🌸 🌸 🌸

In spite of the domineering attitude many Jewish mothers have toward their sons, they always recognize the privilege of the male and acknowledge his intellectual superiority. Their respect for education and learning and their pride in his accomplishment express themselves naïvely. There is the well-known anecdote of the desperate mother who frantically runs along the beach, her arms stretched out to the sea, yelling, "Help! Help! My son, the doctor, is drowning!" The words "my son, the doctor" are almost automatic. That is how the old Jewish woman always speaks of her son. The supreme confidence Jewish mothers have in their sons is beautifully illustrated in a Rothschild anecdote. Once a ghetto neighbor came to the matriarch Gutele Rothschild. There were rumors of an impending war, and the woman, whose son had just reached military age, was worried and anxiously asked Mrs. Rothschild if she had any news if there would be a war. "War? Nonsense!" said Gutele. "My boys won't let them."

Another feature in the characterization of mothers in Jewish wit will become recognizable in the following example: A mother gave her son two neckties as a present. The son, who wanted to show his appreciation, wore one at their next meeting. Noticing it, the mother said, "What's the matter? Don't you like the other one?"

❀ ❀ ❀

The great pianist Arthur Rubinstein once lived in Paris in a district that included the residence of Michael Rubinstein, the successful banker. For several weeks the mail carriers in the neighborhood mixed the two men up and delivered letters to one that were meant for the other and vice versa. Finally Rubinstein, the banker, came over to the home of Rubinstein, the pianist, with a sheaf of letters in his hand. "Please come to my place," said Rubinstein, the banker. "Tell my wife that these notes from Louise of Vienna, Ilsa of Prague, and Margaret of Budapest are addressed to you, not me."

To which Rubinstein, the pianist, replied by extracting a bundle of letters from his desk drawer and saying, "I'll be happy to do that, if you will tell *my* wife that the two million lire in the Bank of Rome and the three million pounds in the Bank of England are yours, not mine."

❀ ❀ ❀

Sonny Teitelbaum came home from med school looking very glum. For three weeks he did nothing but mope in the attic. Then one morning he came down to break-fast and unburdened himself of an awful secret: He had flunked out of med school. "And just because I walked into the wrong room by accident!" His father and mother were of course incensed, and Old Man Teitel-baum got in the Jaguar immediately and drove to the office of the director of the medical college. "I demand—" he spluttered. "My only son! Walked into the wrong room, and flunked out!"

The director suffered a cynical smile to cross his lips. "It sounds like a little thing, doesn't it?" he inquired. "But the fact is, it was a *big* thing. Your son walked into surgery thinking it said autopsy. We found him sawing the leg off a diabetes patient. 'What sort of operation are you performing there, my good man?' I asked him. At that he dropped the scalpel. 'Operation!' he gasped. 'I thought this was a postmortem!' "

☙ ☙ ☙

Dr. Nussbaum was pleased with Mrs. Kaplan's condi-tion. "There seems to be only one problem," he told her after he had finished the examination. "You have a float-ing kidney. But I'm not a bit worried about it."

Mrs. Kaplan, indignant, snapped back, "I wouldn't worry either—if it was *your* kidney!"

☙ ☙ ☙

The Yiddishe Mama

Fanny was sitting at poolside bragging about her grandson Jonathan. "Eighteen months old tomorrow," she was telling her friend Tillie Nickelspan, "and you can't even imagine how smart!"

"Oh, really?" said Tillie. "I suppose he's walking already?"

"Walking?" said Fanny, in a tone that sounded as if she had been insulted. "Why should he walk, when his father owns four Cadillacs!"

🌷 🌷 🌷

Lieb Coleman was comforting his wife, Myrna, who was weeping on his shoulder. "So face it, Myrna," he said tenderly. "We're both old and haven't got much longer to live." This caused more, rather than less, tears and sniffles from the old lady. "And so what if death sometimes strikes without warning, and carries you away before you can even say good-bye?" Now Myrna was really bawling. "*Sha!*" said Lieb sternly. "*Sha,* Myrna! Remember to be brave—always! Should one of us go suddenly, let the other not mourn and carry on, but face the inevitable with courage. More, even! Let the survivor take money out of the bank and not look to the past, but determine to enjoy the future." Now Myrna had calmed down a bit, and Lieb squeezed her shoulder affectionately. Then he murmured, "In fact, darling, should one of us die, I plan to spend a month at the Hilton in Tel Aviv!"

🌷 🌷 🌷

Maxwelton Feigenspahn was ambitious but very poor. His father could not afford to send him through college, so Maxwelton registered at NUY cooperative, which meant that he attended classes for one year at the college and then dropped out the following year and worked in a factory. Under this system, the educational process took eight years, rather than the usual four. But at the end of that time Maxwelton proudly ran home to announce his achievement to Ma and Pa Feigenspahn. He had been granted a degree—from the factory.

❦ ❦ ❦

Montgomery Mishkin went to the hospital and asked to see the nose surgeon. "I want to be a thing of beauty and a *goy* forever, ha-ha-ha," he quipped.

"So-o-o," said the doctor, "you want to cut off your nose to spite your race—"

❦ ❦ ❦

Old Mr. Solomon was giving his daughter some serious advice on the eve of her wedding. "Remember, Sheila," said the old man, "the art of marriage consists always in dividing the responsibilities. The woman has her job cut out for her, and the man has his. Look at your mother and me! Never a quarrel or a cross word between us! Never even a chilling look or a cold shoulder! And do you know why? Because it's like I said, I do my part and she does hers. She takes care of the rent, the utilities bill, the food and clothing, and the raising up of the children. And *I* worry about the important things—the war in Israel, the decline in true religion, and the space program!"

God Bless the Gentiles

My fellow Southerners honor every deed, every gesture, every battered flag, every gravestone that descends from the Civil War. They have conferred sainthood upon every Confederate from Marse Robert himself down to the lowliest drummer boy. They love and cherish them all—all, except one: Judah P. Benjamin, called "the brains of the Confederacy," who served Jeff Davis as Secretary of War and Secretary of State. Not a hurrah—not a word. Nothing. And the interesting thing about this omission is that Benjamin, being a Jew, naturally out-Confederated the Confederates. Only he put it squarely on the line when he said the South was fighting the arbitrary confiscation of private property, Negro slaves.

A few years ago, the Jewish community of Charlotte, North Carolina, wanted to finance a stone marker commemorating Benjamin, which it intended to place on the sidewalk in front of the home he had occupied in the closing days of the war. The United Daughters of the Confederacy said they would go along with this. But then the Daughters balked. A letter had circulated among members of the local Stonewall Jackson Chapter charging that Judah P. Benjamin was a Communist—retro-actively. The Daughters immediately canceled their participation in the ceremony. The Jews scared. They wanted to drop the project. One staunch Daughter, the late Mrs. J. A. Yarborough, remained pro-Benjamin. She insisted. She prevailed. When the Jews told her, "We have to live with these people," Mrs. Yarborough said, "Well, have you given thought to the idea that you'll have to live with me, too?" The marker now stands on South Tryon, Charlotte's main street.

But what kind of Bolshevik was this Judah P. Benjamin? Old Judah was the Tory to end all Tories; he was far, far to the right of both Barry Goldwater and Marie Antoinette.

Right after this incident, I suggested that somewhere during the Sabbath services Jews should repeat a phrase, as part of the creed: *Es vet gornisht helfen* (Nothing helps).

Take the civil rights issue in America—probably as good a jumping-off point for a discussion of anti-Semitism as any. The reason the black man keeps gaining equality is that his movement this time is almost wholly his own. The black wages his own battle, going to the courts, taking to the streets, organizing boycotts. Except for two or three embattled rabbis, the Jews of the South, almost entirely a proprietary class, reflect the total silence of the so-called moderate white Southerners.

But the organ of the States Rights Party of Alabama and Gerald L. K. Smith's hate sheet keep up a constant barrage: "Jews mongrelizing the South." Yet the leading segregationist philosopher of Georgia, the man who de-vised the legal moves to keep colored children out of the

all-white schools, is a Jewish lawyer, Charles Bloch of
Macon. Another influential Jewish segregationist is the
speaker of the South Carolina House of Representatives,
the Honorable Sol Blatt. Does the "states' rights" editor
or Gerald L. K. Smith exempt them? Do they say, "The
Jews are mongrelizing the South except for Charlie
Bloch and Sol Blatt?" They do not.

Es vet gornisht helfen, because the Southern segregationist regards the Jewish white supremacist not as a fellow white Southerner but as a defector from the ranks of
the enemy. He welcomes him with the same reserve he
welcomed the few blacks who inserted an ad in Southern
papers during the mid-fifties with the message: "This is
to inform my white friends I am not now and never have
been a member of the National Association for the Ad-
vancement of Colored People."

I thought of all this after a lecture at Grossinger's in
the Catskill Mountains. During the question period, a
charming lady asked me with some indignation, "Why do
you always talk about civil rights? Don't you know there
are Negro anti-Semites? Besides, what has the Negro ever
done for us?"

I asked her to look about Grossinger's, a wonderful resort that would make the pleasure dome of Xanadu look
like a sharecropper's shack in the Louisiana delta.

"Lady," I answered, "when the Negroes have a
Grossinger's, I'll quit talking about civil rights. And be-
sides, the Negro anti-Semite is about as convincing as the
Jewish white supremacist."

In fact, the segregationists who accept the occasional
Jewish white supremacist hold the black man blameless
for the agitation that is overwhelming the South.

"We understand the Negro," they say. "He is like a child. The Jews put him up to it. The Jews, Earl Warren, and the other Communists."

My first brush with anti-Semitism came when I was a ten-year-old immigrant boy selling newspapers along the Lower East Side of New York City. One day I ventured a block or two beyond our slum into the Irish slum. Some Irish kids chased me, yelling, "Christ killer!"

A year later, three Irish buckoes caught me when I dared a similar venture. They "cockalized" me. There are hundreds of men in their sixties who know what it is to be cockalized. Indeed, cockalization was universal. My father once told me there were specific Polish and Russian words for the process. The enemy kids threw the Jew to the ground, opened his pants, and spat and urinated on his circumcised penis while they shouted, "Christ killer."

Irish, Polish, and Italian kids shouted "Christ killer" because for 1,800 years the church represented the Jews as a people cursed for the crime of crucifying Jesus. Children drank it in with their mother's milk, saw the hatred in action, and heard it confirmed by the prayer on Good Friday, which, until Pope John XXIII deleted it, called the Jews "perfidious."

The ritual of cockalization has disappeared in recent years. One reason is that so many Christian fathers consent to having male offspring circumcised. But the more important reason is that anti-Semitism has had a separate secular career aside from its religious one.

Since the beginning of this century, it has not been necessary to hate the Jew for what he allegedly did 2,000 years ago but for what he might do in the future, which is to take over the world by one or another political or financial stratagem.

As a matter of fact, anti-Semitism has little religious life anymore, thanks to the publication of the *Schema on the Jews,* the Vatican's Ecumenical Council having decided to absolve the Jews from the guilt of having crucified Jesus. The Roman Catholic Church was trying to redress an unjust charge that has cost the lives of millions of people, destroyed millions of homes, and led to enormous expropriation and exploitation.

There is no minimizing the goodwill and nobility of purpose that inspired both Pope John XXIII and Pope Paul VI. For that reason, I sent an open letter to the Jewish leaders of the world calling for a *Jewish* Ecumenical Council in Jerusalem. At the time, the Jews could issue a *Schema on the Christians.*

It is our turn. I propose that we forgive the Christians for the Inquisition, the Crusades, the ghettos, and the expulsions. I think we can also include forgiveness for the usurpation of property that continued for 1,600 years, the worldwide discrimination; we should also waive our annoyances at the barriers that guard country and city, fraternal and luncheon clubs, resort hotels, and college fraternities.

The Christians have been nice. Now *we* can be nice. There is no reason for us to hold bitterness in our hearts because Crusader Godfrey of Bouillon drove the Jews of Jerusalem into the synagogue and set it on fire. There is no reason our Christian neighbors should be held responsible for the wholesale slaughter of the Jews in the cities on the Rhine by the Christians of the Second Crusade. Nor should they be held responsible for the murders perpetrated by Peter the Hermit and Peter of Clugny.

And why should we let the memory of the Inquisition haunt us?

Such a schema will help the cause of brotherhood because the absolution conferred on the Jews by the Ecumenical Council will not mean much to the anti-Semite. Anti-Semitism, according to every authority, has followed a notoriously narrowing career. In the beginning, it led either to conversion or to degradation, but at least it gave the Jew a choice. During some periods of history, conversion made the Jew a preferred citizen. In England, for instance, he lived in Jews' House, where Englishmen fed and clothed him and insisted only that he listen to three Christian sermons a week. From this religious base, anti-Semitism descended to its socioeconomic stage where the dictum ordered, "You cannot live among us." Which meant expulsion. This wasn't a nice choice, but it was still a choice. However, in its twentieth-century political stage, the German Nazis took all the fat out of anti-Semitism. "You cannot live" is no choice at all.

These days, there's not much arguing with the injunction. But then, there was never much arguing to be done with the anti-Semite anyway. The anti-Semite is invariably resourceful. A case in point is Édouard Drumont, editor of *Le Libre Parole*, who spearheaded the French anti-Semitic movement during the Dreyfus affair. When a heckler challenged him, saying, "How can you talk? You married a Jewish woman," Drumont replied, "I hate the Jews for having killed my Lord Jesus, but I love the Jewish women for having wept for Him."

The truth about anti-Semitism is that it is a renunciation of logic, and therefore no logic can prevail against it.

My closest friend, Carl Sandburg, once told me, "Harry, I'll never understand the mystery of anti-Semitism. I've heard it in the wheat fields and in the hobo jungles. I've heard it around the campfires in Puerto Rico during the Spanish-American War, and I've heard it in the union halls. I've heard it among the fellow Socialists and among fellow poets. I've heard it among the poor looking for a handout, and I've heard it among the rich, the powerful, and the intellectual. It remains for me a great mystery."

This may help explain why many American Jews often express a day-to-day concern over anti-Semitism. No matter how good things are, no matter how deep the involvement of some Jews in politics, others in philanthropy, still others in civic works, anti-Semitism remains an ill-defined, yet frequently present menace for Jews, and this despite the fact that American Jews are guaranteed political and religious liberty.

Nor does the Jew's concern—or may I call it fear?—abate when anti-Semitism issues only from the mouths of obviously discredited hatemongers such as George Lincoln Rockwell and Gerald L. K. Smith. The Jew is doubly exposed. He is exposed as a Jew, a marginal member of society, and he is exposed because so many of his numbers are now in the middle class, and the congenital disease of the middle class itself is fear. *This month is good. But what about next month? Will we meet the quota?*

Knowing this, I have often wondered why my fellow Jews did not take advantage of middle-class status to end anti-Semitism. In fact, I offered the Golden Plan to End Anti-Semitism to the Anti-Defamation League some years ago. I urged them to insert a full-page ad in every morning and evening newspaper, every weekly and monthly magazine in America. The ad would declare in effect that the next time we heard any anti-Semitism, we all would become Christians immediately. Most of us, I am sure, would naturally head for the High Episcopal Church, and the prospect of several million Jews entering such Fifth Avenue institutions as the Church of the Heavenly Rest or St. Thomas' would make the Episcopalians plenty nervous. They might even volunteer to support the Anti-Defamation League and establish a truly influential phalanx against the anti-Semites.

The ADL did not take me up on this plan, but that's because they thought I was kidding.

Only this kind of magic will banish anti-Semitism, because anti-Semitism is also a powerful magic. In the hands of a demagogue, it works better than magic.

It enabled Hitler to convert economic and political misery into the hatred of "the conspirators" who wrought the misery. It does not alleviate the misery, but it convinces people that if they search out the enemy, the misery will go away of its own accord. The Germans hated the Versailles Treaty; they hated the inflation and the unemployment conditions for which there were not any viable short-range solutions. But anti-Semitism cuts through the economic and political and historical abstractions and pins a faceless, ubiquitous enemy to the wall. Thus the Nazis found the devil who caused their troubles: the Jew.

This is not a process Hitler invented. Anti-Semites have a natural facility for this maneuver. Dear reader, let's face it—anti-Semitism cannot possibly be explained; it can merely be recounted.

In 1913, Tom Watson of Georgia, an old Populist who

was then out of elective office, regained political power
with the anti-Semitism he poured forth in his newspaper,
The Weekly Jeffersonian. Georgia was literally destitute.
The price of cotton had dropped to five cents a pound.
Farmers burned it for fuel. The average wage in the mill
villages was twenty cents an hour for an eleven-hour day.
Then on Confederate Memorial Day, April 26, 1913,
someone murdered a little factory girl named Mary Phagan. The police arrested her boss, Leo Frank, the super-
intendent of the National Pencil Company, the last man
to see Mary alive, when she had come that Saturday noon
to collect her pay. Leo Frank, in Tom Watson's hands,
soon became the symbol of everything that oppressed
Georgia. He was the Northern employer, the Jewish cap-
italist, the college-educated snob who desecrated virgins.
That Frank was innocent made no difference; that his
trial judge doubted his guilt, that two justices of the
Georgia Court of Appeals doubted, that Justices Holmes
and Hughes of the United States Supreme Court
doubted, that Governor John Slaton doubted to the degree that he commuted the sentence made no difference.

Whipped on by the talented polemics of Watson, a
well-trained band of men calling themselves the Knights
of Mary Phagan broke into the Milledgeville Prison,
seized Frank, drove him 170 miles over backwoods roads,
and hanged him from an oak tree near the house in
which Mary Phagan had been born. Tom Watson also
sparked the only European-type pogrom America has ex-
perienced. A boycott of epidemic proportions drove 100
Jewish families from Georgia. Physical intimidation of
Jews was commonplace for the next few years.

Tom Watson of Georgia is an excellent example of the
factors involved that make a man an anti-Semite: an alco-

holic with a hacking cough; a politician whose influence wanes; a small merchant for whom the competition is too tough; the fellow who can't keep a decent job. Give him the panacea—anti-Semitism—and each is on his way. As an active anti-Semite he suddenly feels an attachment for a cause as old as history itself. Yesterday he was a nobody; today he is a warrior ready to do battle for mankind against a "shrewd" eternal race.

And why the Jews?

There are Jews who have assayed better answers than I can offer. Shmyra Levin wrote, "Where planes meet, friction begins." The Jews and the Christians "met" long ago. The Jew bears an identity with every step of the Christians' way: with his birth, his marriage, his church, and his death. The Jew is identified with the man on the cross, *his* birth, *his* death, *his* second coming, and with the life everlasting.

Chaim Weizmann said, "We are a cinder in their eye." And Sigmund Freud, expanding on his theory of the Oedipus complex, theorized: "The Jews had a father religion and the Christians a son religion and the subconscious wish is to kill the father from time to time."

In discussing the origins of modern anti-Semitism, Miriam Beard suggests that the mythical Nordic innocents of the pre-Jewish, premercantile era were thought of as "swashbuckling D'Artagnans scattering louis d'or without thought of the morrow . . . indeed, the burden of guilt (of inventing capitalism) was laid upon the Jew who was supposed to have misled the gentiles away from the Table Round to the stock market."

There is the apocryphal story of the anti-Semitic poster nailed to the bulletin board of a Vienna steel factory that detailed all the troubles the Jews had caused. Commented one worker to another with a shrug, "There'll be another wage cut on Monday."

Nor must we forget the value of anti-Semitism as a gauge of self-respect and proof of individual worth to the genteel middle class and poor. Jean-Paul Sartre believes the Dreyfus case was a boon to the bourgeoisie of France: ". . . it opened the doors of the aristocracy to them." A Frenchman would say, "I am no janitor, I'm an anti-Dreyfusard!"

Let's talk about these "social" restrictions for a moment. In Charlotte, for example, the grandson of a Jewish merchant who donated money to help the city pay its schoolteachers during an economic crisis in the 1870's cannot join the City (luncheon) Club, but a newly arrived (Gentile) branch manager from Ohio is immediately welcomed with open arms. This situation exists throughout the country, and there's more to it than the usual excuse that the country club and the "downtown" luncheon club are private organizations. We are a socially oriented society. The contract for the new school is discussed over lunch at this "exclusive" club; the City Council often meets there, and the artist in town for a concert that evening is entertained there. But much more is involved. I had a bit of a grant in 1950 to study this problem. I spoke with managing directors of a number of major corporations, all of whom employ Jews in their research, engineering and sales departments—in the metropolitan areas. They did not say as much, but I was left with the unmistakable impression that they would not promote a Jew to a regional managerial position, no matter how qualified and deserving. Such a position requires total social integration at the local level —the country club, the downtown club, the entertaining at one another's homes—and a wife who would be socially acceptable immediately.

I do not know how it is in other parts of the country, but in the South the wife is the key to this complete social acceptance. This enables the Southerner to move through two worlds, one populated by ordinary creatures and one populated by his wife. He need never commit himself socially with the people he meets unless he commits his wife. I have known Jewish merchants in the South with a record of business success and civic works who have lived in their community for more than a quarter of a century in good fellowship with their fellow Gentile businessmen but who have never met their wives.

I recall a question I once put to a Christian missionary whose denomination supported a Mission to the Jews. I asked him how come he and his fellow missionaries were so anxious to save me, to have me join them in heaven through all eternity, but they wouldn't let me join the City Club where I'd come only once or twice a month for a comparatively limited number of years.

All this is not as sad as it sounds, because the restrictions do tend to accelerate the Jew's competitive drive. The poet Heine said it over a century ago: "We must be twice as good to get half as much." And it should be remembered, too, that in America these restrictions have never been sanctioned by either law or public opinion.

These restrictions grew up in snobbery. Anyone can trace the vein of anti-Semitism that ran through American literature in the 1920's. That vein was nourished by such antipathy as collected around aliens such as Sacco and Vanzetti; it was fed by Mitchell Palmer, the Attorney General who arrested and deported radical foreign-

ers by the boatload; by the Ku Klux Klan, which redefined America as containing only white Protestants of
northern European origin.

Forty years ago, some of our most famous writers felt
that the threat of the Jews was not to the true faith or to
the pocketbook but to the social structure. The Nobel
Prizewinning poet T. S. Eliot was one of the pioneers in
the expression of genteel anti-Semitism. In his well-known
poem "Burbank with a Baedeker: Bleistein with a
Cigar," Eliot complains not that Bleistein is a Jew but
that he has pretensions to culture in a world wracked by
social disorder and instability. It dismays him that a Chicago "Semite" invades the museum to gape at a painting
by Canaletto.

Ernest Hemingway and F. Scott Fitzgerald, who could
not agree why the rich were different from the rest of us,
did agree on the Jew. Robert Cohn of *The Sun Also
Rises* and Meyer Wolfsheim of *The Great Gatsby* are no
doubt genuine literary creations, but they are also dehu-
manized figures, deliberately graceless, with no compas-
sion offered.

But if we are to isolate the disease of anti-Semitism, we
cannot locate it by an examination of the Jew. It is the
anti-Semite who is sick, misinformed, hateful, and unfair.
Not to mention, humorless. Anti-Semitism is isolated in
the mind of the anti-Semite, the man whom Eric Hoffer
called the "hitchhiker of mankind" in his little treatise
The True Believer. To this "hitchhiker," anti-Semitism
offers an immediate hope of help, as well as a sense of participation in something as important as saving the world.

Perhaps most important of all inspirations, the anti-
Semite often burns with a consuming hatred of Jesus,
which he prudently expresses against the people who pro-

duced him. Hating Jews also allows the anti-Semite to strike blows against the restricting ethics of Christianity without risking his standing in the community.

There are other reasons why men become anti-Semites. It is nearly always profitable. Whole duchies once existed on a Jewish "life" tax and on periodic confiscations of Jewish property. Some men have become anti-Semites because their teeth hurt, or because they are sexually impotent, or because they are just plain insane. But whether insane or opportunists, they are always alert to the "devil" of the moment, the devil who has just invested the Jews. In this decade, of course, that devil is Bolshevism.

A century ago, and even less, counting Tom Watson, the devil was capitalism. Brooks Adams never recovered from his melancholia induced by the Jews because they "invented" money and thus "gave rise to the bourgeoisie that destroyed the world of priests, knights, peasants and artisans." Hugh Dorsey, who prosecuted Leo Frank, asked the defendant's mother, "Is it not true you own stocks and bonds on Wall Street?" The devil of capitalism invested Jews for more than a century.

A famous Southern tent evangelist, the Reverend Mordecai Ham, lived long enough to embrace both ends of modern anti-Semitism. In the early 1920's the evangelist inveighed against Jewish "international bankers," and in the 1940's old Ham charged the same Jewish "international bankers" with conspiring to destroy free enterprise.

In reaction to all this, the modern Jew has almost always thrown himself into the struggle for liberal causes, because the Jew believes the liberal cause he espouses at the moment will benefit the general population. He

wants the Gentile to have more and more peace of mind
—Social Security, hospital insurance, full employment
and pensions, a dozen TVA's if necessary.

The Jew knows that the state of the economy is an important factor in the rise and fall of anti-Semitism. In
Russia the pogroms came at a period of almost unbelievable poverty of the peasant; in France in the 1890's it was
the disaster following military defeat and the depression
following the Panama Canal swindles; in Germany it was
the defeat of the war machine in 1918, the inflation, and
the economic collapse. And in the state of Georgia in
1913 it was the poverty of the tenant farmers and the
frustration of the mill hand who was getting twenty cents
an hour in the cotton mills, the state of the economy, and
the mental state of the individual anti-Semite.

But this is *our* big advantage. The anti-Semite, no matter how talented, must pray that his country and its people meet with some major disaster—plague, famine, economic disruption or military defeat—otherwise he talks
into the wind, even if he's as talented as Hitler, Watson,
or Drumont.

At a convention of the Episcopal Society for Cultural
and Racial Unity, which I addressed in Chicago, I told
the delegates: "You may not know it, but there are five
and a half million Jews in America praying for you fellows every day. They don't go into synagogues and pray,
but I believe most of them somehow utter a prayer for
you, hope that your children are healthy, that you remain prosperous and that you never have bad luck. Because when the Gentile is in trouble, the Jew catches
hell."

The Jew knows the anti-Semite can give him hell and
still retain and perhaps enlarge his standing in the com-

munity. While anti-Semitism has never been as respectable in America as it has been in Europe, no one goes to jail for it.

Well, no one asks a man to love a Jew simply because he is a Jew. That is a bargain not much better than anti-Semitism. That is not the point at all. As Isaac Babel, the Jewish writer, once remarked, it is impossible to live without enemies. The point is that the anti-Semite's sole purpose in life is to do harm to other human beings—men, women, and children indiscriminately, because they happen to be Jewish, men, women and children who never did him any harm, whom he does not even know.

But the anti-Semite who wishes to remain civilized can do so in only one way: He must renounce his religious creed that descends from one of the Semitic religions—Judaism, Christianity, or Islam—and he must dispense with the clergyman's last words over his remains: "How goodly are thy tents O Jacob," if a Protestant, and "Into the bosom of Abraham," if a Catholic.

He should live so long.

You Should See Her Pictures

TWO Jews met at a convention, and the following is their conversation:

"Where are you from?"

"I am from Charlotte, North Carolina."

"Charlotte, North Carolina? How many Jews are there in Charlotte?"

"About three thousand Jews."

"That's a good-sized Jewish community. And how many Gentiles are there?"

"Gentiles we have plenty; about two hundred and fifty thousand."

"Two hundred and fifty thousand? You need that many?"

❦ ❦ ❦

It is the year 2001, and of course the blacks have taken over. The President, Vice President, and all the members of the Cabinet are black, and at a Cabinet meeting the janitor is a Jew. He keeps sweeping up the Cabinet

Room, the cigarette butts, and papers, and all the time he's humming the tune "Have Negilah." The Secretary of State leans over to the President and says, "One thing about them Jews, they sure have rhythm."

🌷 🌷 🌷

Down through history there have always been bigots who will not support a Jew for public office. Disraeli encountered one when he first ran for Parliament. When he solicited the anti-Semite's vote, the man hissed, "I would rather vote for the devil himself than vote for you."

"I understand perfectly," countered Disraeli in an even voice. "But in case your friend decides not to run, may I count on your support?"

🌷 🌷 🌷

Mrs. Levine, her face wreathed in proud smiles, was pushing her baby carriage along Wilshire Boulevard in Los Angeles, taking her infant daughter on her first outing. On the way she encountered a neighbor, who gushed over the baby.

"What a beautiful child!" the neighbor cried.

Mrs. Levine smiled delightedly. "This is nothing," she boasted. "You should see her pictures!"

🌷 🌷 🌷

You Should See Her Pictures

Dr. Albert Einstein told of the time the late Mayor LaGuardia of New York became ill with an intestinal disorder. While recuperating at Montefiore Hospital, he received a resolution from the powers-that-be: "The City Council wishes you quick recovery by a vote of 19 to 12."

❦ ❦ ❦

Around the turn of the century, when the Jews of New York were fighting for the right to organize their labor unions and the ensuing strife created much ferment and antagonisms, the police often used their clubs to crack the skulls of the striking garment workers. The epithet "Cossack!" was frequently applied to the officers, many of whom were anti-Semitic. Following is a popular joke of the late 1890's and the first decade of this century.

A police officer passed by a home in which a circumcision had just been performed. As he watched, the *mohel,* whom the policeman knew, came out of the house.

"Hey, butcher, tell me something," said the officer jeeringly. "What do you do with all the pieces you cut off?"

"I'll be glad to tell you," answered the *mohel* courteously. "I send them downtown where they make cops out of them!"

❦ ❦ ❦

"The Jews in America are reported to be so fancy," said the sage of a small Ukrainian village, "that when the *mohel* circumcises an infant, he uses pinking shears!"

135

"My second wife divorced me because of illness. She got sick of me!"

🌷 🌷 🌷

In the days of Czar Nicholas, a friendly Jew boarded a train for Minsk. Opposite him, in the same compartment, sat a lieutenant of the czarist army with a small dog on his lap.

The amiable Jew attempted to strike up a conversation, but the Russian officer gave him such a withering look that he hastily retreated into silence.

But the lieutenant, not satisfied with silencing the hated Jew, kept stroking his dog and all the while maliciously calling the animal "Isaac."

Finally the Jewish traveler had enough. "It's too bad about your dog," he remarked innocently.

"What's too bad about him?" snapped the lieutenant.

"That he has a Jewish name."

"I still don't know what you are talking about."

"Well, if it weren't for his Jewish name," the little man explained politely, "he might someday be a lieutenant like his master."

🌷 🌷 🌷

A general was talking to the late Albert Einstein.

"Our losses in the last military campaign were relatively mild," the army officer commented with deep pride.

"Relative to *what?*" asked the inventor of the theory.

❦ ❦ ❦

A German entered a streetcar and, because there were no other seats available, had no alternative but to sit beside a Jew.

"I can see by your nose that you are a filthy Jew," said the venomous German. "Every thought in your head is concentrated on defiling blond Aryan girls."

The Jew ignored him, studiously fixing his gaze in another direction.

After a few minutes, the German broke the silence. "What time is it, Jew?"

The Jew did not answer.

"I asked you a question—what time is it?"

No reply.

"Listen, Jew, I'm asking you for the last time—what time is it? What's the matter with you, are you deaf?"

"No, I am not deaf," the Jew answered at last. "But if you can tell my sexual preferences by looking at my nose, you certainly should be able to tell the time by looking at the watch in my pocket!"

❦ ❦ ❦

During the last days of the reign of cruel Czar Nicholas, a Jew fell into the Moskva River and was in imminent danger of drowning.

"Help! Help! I can't swim!" screamed the terror-stricken Jew.

A squad of the czar's soldiers, loitering on the bank, laughed derisively, making no move to help the doomed man.

"Save me!" bellowed the poor soul again. But the soldiers only laughed louder.

"Down with the czar—up with the revolution!" screamed the nimble-witted Jew hoarsely as he was going under for the third time.

The soldiers immediately jumped into the river and dragged the man to safety.

"We'll teach you to defame the sacred name of the czar," they roared as they hauled the grinning Jew to jail.

🌷 🌷 🌷

Paul Muni, famed actor of the Yiddish and American stage and cinema, bought his wife a new car. Asked how she liked it, he replied, "She loves to drive! My wife now has two hundred and fifty horses that can take her through ten city streets of solid concrete, from our house to the supermarket, and then all the way back home, in a two-ton vehicle, just to transport four ounces of pastrami."

🌷 🌷 🌷

A badly frightened Jew stood before the bar of "justice" in a German court.

"The charge against you is very serious," intoned the judge. "You are accused of maligning the Nazi Party—the government itself."

"B-b-but, Your Honor," stammered the Jew, "I was referring to the Communists, not the Nazis."

"Don't lie to me!" spat the magistrate. "The indictment accused you of using the words 'murderers, gangsters, and thieves.' This court knows exactly whom you meant!"

🌷 🌷 🌷

Ignace J. Paderewski, post-World War I Premier of Poland, was discussing his country's affairs with then President, Woodrow Wilson.

"If all of Poland's demands are not granted at the peace conference," warned Paderewski, "I can foresee serious trouble to my country. Why, my people will be so angry that many of them will go out and massacre the Jews."

"And what will happen if we meet your demands?" asked Wilson.

"Why, my people will be so happy," replied the Premier, "that many of them will get drunk and go out and massacre the Jews."

🌷 🌷 🌷

A German Jew was in a public park, sitting on a yellow-painted bench reserved for the "inferior race." He was absorbed in his newspaper, the Zionist weekly, *Jüdische Rundschau,* and it was some moments before he realized that a Jewish acquaintance had also sat down on the bench and was reading Julius Streicher's *Stürmer.*

"I'm surprised at you," said the first Jew indignantly. "How can a Jew bring himself to read such anti-Semitic garbage?"

"To tell you the truth, it gives me a small measure of comfort," replied the other.

"Comfort? How can you derive any comfort from such a rag?"

"Let me explain. When I read *Rundschau* I am told of pogroms in Poland, of persecution here in Germany, of terrorism in Palestine, and other such happenings which depress me. But when I read Streicher's *Stürmer* I am told that the Jews are international bankers, that they control the press, that they dominate business—all this gives my morale a tremendous lift!"

🌱 🌱 🌱

RASPUTIN: Your Majesty, the Jews are saying you are anti-Semitic. Why not kill them all as a lesson?

CZAR NICHOLAS: Whoever said I was anti-Semitic is a liar. And to prove it, I certainly will not kill them all as you suggest. You should be ashamed of yourself for even thinking such terrible things. Kill half!

🌱 🌱 🌱

Moses Greenspahn read an advertisement that a certain publishing house in Berlin needed a proofreader, and he applied for the job.

"We don't employ Jews here," said the foreman. "However, if you'll agree to be baptized, I might make an exception in your case."

"Oh, no," replied Greenspahn, "I could never do that."

"Then get out," snapped the foreman. "As long as I am alive, no Jew will ever be employed by this firm."

"I'll wait," said Greenspahn.

🌷 🌷 🌷

Adolf Cohen went to the Berlin Municipal Court to change his name legally. When his case came up, the judge took one look at the application, another at the petitioner, and flew into a rage.

"What is this, another of your Jewish tricks?" he ranted. "Do you think that the Third Reich will permit you to hide your Jewish blood behind an Aryan name? Get out of this court. Your name is Cohen, and Cohen it will remain!"

"But, Your Honor," protested the Jew, "I am perfectly satisfied with that part of my name. I only want to change Adolf to Abraham!"

🌷 🌷 🌷

Albert Einstein, guest of honor at an intercollegiate banquet of his peers, was describing conditions in Nazi Germany. The dean of Harvard interrupted.

"Dr. Einstein, I cannot understand how Germany, a nation that was foremost among the liberal arts and sciences, could have succumbed to the anti-intellectualism of Nazi philosophy. What in the world happened there?"

"I'll tell you what happened," replied Einstein. "The German people were imbued with three qualities: honesty, intelligence, and Nazism. However, our Creator, in His wisdom, decreed that because we mortals are partly creatures of freewill, a German could only possess two of the three qualities. That is why a German who is honest and also a Nazi cannot be intelligent. If he is intelligent and a Nazi, he cannot be honest. And if he is honest and intelligent, he cannot be a Nazi."

❀ ❀ ❀

The grand rabbi of Bucharest first said it:

"The division between man and woman is not as important as the multiplication."

❀ ❀ ❀

For many years the stereotype went something like this: "The Jews are traders and businessmen, but they are poor fighters."

You Should See Her Pictures

Now, with the survival of an Israel surrounded by enemies, and the conquest of the Sinai Peninsula in three days—but with a sidelong glance at Israel's unbalanced budget—all this may be changed: "Them Jews are great fighters, but they are certainly poor businessmen."

🌷 🌷 🌷

Once there was a rabbi who wasn't doing too well. He decided to go into some kind of business in order to make a living. He decided to become a fish peddler. His wife prepared the fish for him. He sold both gefilte and fried fish, and he also had horseradish on his cart because everyone knew that fish had to be eaten with horseradish. He chose a fine place to sell his fish, right across the street from the largest bank in the city. Another rabbi happened to see him selling fish and wished him lots of luck. He then asked him if he could lend him five rubles. Now, our fish-selling friend was really in a pickle. He didn't want to lend out five rubles, but he didn't want to refuse his friend either. After a short interlude, he replied, "You know, I'd be more than willing to lend you the five rubles, but I've made a deal with the bank across the street. They promised not to sell any fish if I didn't make any loans."

🌷 🌷 🌷

A ship was once at sea. All at once a terrible storm broke out. There was truly a great danger to the passen-

gers on board. The ship was tossed violently in the water.
Women soon began to faint, and men cried bitter tears.
One Jew on board was carrying on so fiercely that he
was beside himself. *"Oy,"* he cried, "the ship is sinking!
Oy, the ship will break into a thousand pieces."

Another Jew was very puzzled by the attitude of his
fellow traveler. He went over to him and said, "Why are
you carrying on, is it your ship?"

❦ ❦ ❦

Two Jews once got into a violent argument. Finally
one challenged the other to a duel. Both had been soldiers, and both could shoot well. They decided to meet at
six the next morning. At six, one of the two arrived. He
waited for half an hour, and the other still hadn't shown
up. Just then a messenger arrived with a note from the
other. It read as follows: "Joe, I'll be late tomorrow.
Don't wait—shoot without me."

❦ ❦ ❦

A Jewish soldier once left the front AWOL. He was
caught in a small town nearby. The soldiers dragged him
to the commanding officer, who noticed that this fellow
was a very healthy, strong young man. "Aren't you
ashamed of yourself, deserting the front? Weaker men
than you didn't desert. And furthermore, you took an
oath to be true to his majesty, the czar."

The Jew answered, "Your honor, really, I am a true soldier, that's why I went AWOL."

❦ ❦ ❦

A bearded Jew, a venerable-looking patriarch, was arrested for imbibing too freely in public and was hauled before a judge.

"Grandfather," the magistrate admonished, "how could a respectable old gentleman like you be found intoxicated in the street?"

"It's a lie, a conspiracy of the Police Department. I was not drunk then, and I am not drunk now!"

"Look at you, you're weaving and staggering so you can scarcely stand. How did you ever happen to get in this condition?"

"Actually it is all quite simple," answered the ancient one. "I started out with the intention of taking only one drink. It was enough—I was satisfied. But that one drink made a new man of me, and the new man wanted a drink, too. After all, he was entitled, and when a man is entitled, he's entitled, and that's all there is to it. So he had his drink. Now there were two of us, yes? One and one is two. Now, Your Honor, everyone knows that when two Jews get together, it is permissible that they share a little schnapps. Look it up in the Torah. Anyway, we made a few little toasts to each other, and by this time we were both feeling joyous. And that's the whole point, Your Honor. On a joyous occasion a Jew is *supposed* to drink!"

145

In nearly all the collections of humor there are no jokes about honeymoons—Jews did not have honeymoons. There are no jokes about maternity suits or homosexuals, but plenty of jokes about women. The predominant figures in Yiddish humor remain the same: the *shnorrer* (panhandler); the *gvir* (rich man); the *poyer* (peasant); the *poretz* (feudal baron); and of course the *balagoola* (ignoramus).

❀ ❀ ❀

From the Talmud:
"Instead of breaking bones at Abaye's, come rather to Raba, in order to eat fat meat."

"Only small change rattles in the pocket."

"The table is there, also the meat and the water; we lack only the mouth in order to be able to eat."

"If anyone says to you: 'Your friend is dead,' believe it; if he says to you: 'He has become rich,' believe it not."

"Dying is easier than getting rich."

"Audacity is effective even with God."

"When the thief lacks opportunity, he is condemned to honesty."

"The robber knows his own handiwork."

"If thou wilt hang thyself, do it on a high tree."

You Should See Her Pictures

🌷 🌷 🌷

It is said that Hitler, disturbed by nightmares, called in a soothsayer.

The seer consulted a crystal ball and said, "Ah, mighty *Führer*, it is foretold that you will die on a Jewish holiday."

"Which one?" scowled Hitler.

"Any day you die will be a Jewish holiday."

🌷 🌷 🌷

Three fellows were playing pinochle in the courthouse in Russia. One was a Russian, one a Pole, and one a Jew. This act under Russian law was considered extremely improper. The three were caught and taken to a police station. They all of course denied their guilt. The police officer wanted them all to take an oath. The Russian and the Pole swore on the spot that they were innocent. But the Jew didn't think so lightly of a false oath. So he said to the officer, "*Nu*, why should I swear, how could I have played three-handed pinochle by myself?"

🌷 🌷 🌷

A Jewish woman not known for her piety went to *shul* on Yom Kippur just like everyone else. She remained

147

there throughout the day. However, although all the other women cried throughout the services, she only prayed. One woman asked her, "Why weren't you crying? Have you sinned less than any of us?"

Hannah replied, "I know I've committed a lot of sins, but I'm sure God will forgive me."

"Why are you so sure?"

Hannah answered, "Even a thief would have mercy if you would beg and plead with him for a whole day."

(*)

🌼 🌼 🌼

A group of people were being led to jail. Among them were a number of Jews. A group of Jewish women were standing nearby, shaking their heads. They asked one, "Why are you being led away?"

He answered, "Because I didn't have a passport."

The women began to cry, "They're taking him away because he didn't have a passport, how terrible!" They asked a second man, "Why are you being taken to prison?"

He answered, "I evaded military service."

"Military service," they repeated. "How awful!" And they began to cry again.

They asked a third man, a young, very well-built fellow. He answered, "I'm only a thief."

🌼 🌼 🌼

You Should See Her Pictures

The migration of the Jews, especially those forced to emigrate by persecution, has become the subject of many jokes since Hitler. Here is an example from the time when Hitler entered Austria. A Jew asked the advice of the travel office about where he could immigrate. The clerk and he considered the various countries as possibilities and realized that the entrance into each was beset with difficulties. In one country you needed a certain amount of money for entry, in another a labor permit or a certificate of employment. For another country the passport had no validity; a fourth land did not want any immigrants, and so on. While the two men thus considered the various countries, they whirled the globe near the desk. Finally the desperate Jew asked, "Haven't you got another globe?"

🌷 🌷 🌷

One of the best advertisements I've ever seen is a sign in a surgical appliance store on Delancey Street which reads: *Your killa is my gedillah.* (Your rupture is my rapture.)

🌷 🌷 🌷

There was a big to-do in Charlotte a few months ago. Several young girls were attacked during the night, and since they could not apprehend the criminal, the rumor got around that it was a vampire because of the marks on the necks of the girls. How Dracula got from the Carpathian mountains to Charlotte is a mystery, and why it should attack in Charlotte, North Carolina, is an even greater mystery. However, he gave himself away one night when he stole into a young girl's bedroom. The girl was asleep, and so this Dracula threw his black cape behind him, kneeled down beside the girl's bed, and began to suck her neck for the blood. She raised herself pretty quickly and grabbed a protective crucifix from her night table and started to wave it in front of Dracula. However, Dracula stepped back, and he said, "Who-Ha, lady, do you hev the wrong wempire?"

🌷 🌷 🌷

Two GI's in Honolulu went into a Chinese laundry; one of the men had left his shirts there. The laundryman wanted a ticket which the GI did not have. After arguing for some time, the GI went behind the counter, ripped open a few packages, and found his shirts. He satisfied the laundryman that those were his shirts, paid his bill, and went out. Still angry over the argument he had had with the laundryman, the GI kept repeating, "That lousy Jew."

His companion said, "That was no Jew; that's a Chinaman."

And the GI replied: "Them's the worst kind."

The Jews Already Had Diabetes

TWO fellows met at Katz's delicatessen store every noon; week after week they ate their sandwiches without saying a word to each other. Finally the patience of one fellow ran out, and he said, "Jake, we've been coming in here for two years every day at noon, we eat a sandwich and never say a word to each other; why don't you at least ask me how's business?"

So the other one answered: "So how's business?" and the answer was: "Don't ask!"

🌷 🌷 🌷

While the Anglo-Saxons were still roaming the fields of Great Britain painting their bodies blue and eating berries, we Jews already had diabetes.

🌷 🌷 🌷

Two fellows went into a swell restaurant by mistake, and they had lunch, and at the end of the lunch, the waiter brought them the finger bowls. They looked at the finger bowls and then looked at each other with a quizzical look on their faces. "What's this?"

"The soup, we had, and this is no tea, so what's this? Let's ask the waiter."

"No, you ask him."

"All right. So, waiter, come over here. The soup we had, and this isn't tea, so what's this?"

So the waiter answered, "Those are finger bowls; when you get through with your lunch, you dip your fingers in them."

"See—you ask a foolish question you get a foolish answer!"

❦ ❦ ❦

Willie Johnson invited his little Jewish friend Izzie to attend the Sunday school class at the local Baptist church. The subject for that day was "love," and in order to arouse the interest of her pupils, the teacher offered a prize of twenty-five cents to the child whose answers were most correct.

"Whom does our religion teach us to love above all others?" the teacher asked, opening the class discussion.

"Our mothers," said a little girl.

"Our fathers," said Willie Johnson.

The teacher shook her head. "It is true that our religion teaches us to love our parents," she said, "but there is one other whom we must love even more."

"George Washington?" asked one of the boys.

"Abraham Lincoln!"

The Jewish boy raised his hand. "I know the answer," he said. "You mean Jesus Christ."

"Correct!" exclaimed the teacher. "Step forward and get your twenty-five cents. What's your name?"

"Izzie Eisenstein."

"Aren't you Jewish?"

"Yes, ma'am."

"Why, I think it is marvelous that even a Jewish boy knows we must love Jesus above everybody else. How did you happen to think of it, young man?"

"Well, lady, actually I thought of Moses," muttered Izzie, pocketing the twenty-five cents, "but business is business."

🌷 🌷 🌷

Max was caught red-handed by a police officer in the very act of burglarizing a store. He was quickly brought to trial.

"How do you plead?" asked the judge.

"Your Honor," answered Max, "before I plead guilty or not guilty, I ask that the court kindly appoint a lawyer to defend me."

"Max, you were caught in the actual commission of a crime. What could any lawyer possibly say in your defense?"

"That's exactly my point, Your Honor," said Max. "I'm curious also to hear what he could possibly say!"

A rich man was enjoying the company of the celebrated wit Herschel Ostropollier.

"Herschel," he said, "if you can tell me a really spontaneous lie—without thinking—I'll give you a ruble."

Herschel's answer was instantaneous. "What do you mean, one ruble—you just said *two!*"

🌷 🌷 🌷

"My wife divorced me for religious reasons. She worshiped money, and I didn't have any!"

🌷 🌷 🌷

A well-to-do American Jew who had spent many years in a small town moved to the city and was made chairman of the ritual committee of a large synagogue. Before the High Holy Days it was his duty to engage a cantor. When the transaction was completed, the cantor inquired, "How about a *shofar?*"

"Look, mister, you may be a great cantor, but don't put on any airs with me," snapped the new chairman. "If I, a rich man, can drive my own car, then so can you— and without a *chauffeur!*"

🌷 🌷 🌷

The Jews Already Had Diabetes

A poor Jewish farmer called on his affluent neighbor to borrow his donkey.

"I'm sorry, neighbor, but my donkey is in the next pasture right now," said the rich farmer.

At that moment the hee-haw of a jackass was heard, braying in the nearby stable.

"Your alibi wasn't very clever," said the poor man bitterly.

The well-to-do farmer made a show of being offended. "Now look, neighbor," he asked with dignity, "whom are you going to believe? Me or a braying ass?"

❦ ❦ ❦

A man walked into the tailor shop on Rivington Street to get his suit pressed.

"That will be two dollars," said the tailor.

"Two dollars!" cried the customer, outraged. "Why, back in Minsk I could get my suit pressed for twenty-five cents!"

"That I believe," said the tailor coolly, "but look at the fare!"

❦ ❦ ❦

STUDENT: Rabbi, why did God make man before woman?
RABBI: Because He didn't want any advice on how to make a man!

157

A great king, grown old and eccentric, called before him the chief rabbi of his realm. "Before I die, there's something I want you to do, Rabbi. Teach my pet monkey how to talk!"

"What?"

"That's a command: Teach my monkey how to talk, within one year, or your head will be chopped off!"

"But, Your Majesty, to carry out a request like that, I need more than a year—I need at least ten."

"I'll allow you five and not a day more!"

The rabbi returned to his flock and told them what had happened. And they all cried out in sympathy, "But what will you *do, rov?*"

"Well," said the *rov,* "in five years, many things can happen. For instance, the king could die. Or I could die. Or—the monkey could die. And besides, in five years, who knows—maybe I can teach that monkey how to talk!"

(Leo Rosten)

❁ ❁ ❁

George S. Kaufman, a prince of wit, once remarked that he liked to write with his collaborator Moss Hart because Hart was so lucky. "In my case," said Kaufman, "it's *gelt* by association."

❁ ❁ ❁

The Jews Already Had Diabetes

A Jew was once found eating on the Fast of Gedaliah, a minor fast day. This incident was immediately reported to the rabbi. The rabbi asked to speak to him, and the *apikoros* came willingly. "How is it," said the rabbi, "that you eat on this fast day?"

The free thinker responded, "First it was postponed because of Shabbas, and since we can't fast on Shabbas, I didn't want to fast on Sunday. Second, if Gedaliah hadn't been assassinated, he would have died anyway. Third, if I would have been killed, would Gedaliah have fasted for me? And fourth, if I eat on Yom Kippur, why should I fast on the Fast of Gedaliah?"

❁ ❁ ❁

Two Jews were walking on the street. Both were unfortunately very hungry. On the street they spotted a bagel. Both jumped at the bagel and tried to grab it. Each screamed that he had found it first. However, they finally decided it would be silly to fight over a bagel, and they agreed that each would go to sleep and that the one who had the nicest dream would get the bagel. Both slept and woke up about an hour later. One began to tell the other about his dream. "I dreamed that I was carried by a large white dove who flew me right into the Garden of Eden," said one.

"You know," said the other one, "I had the same dream about you: The white dove flew you right to the Garden of Eden. So you know what I did since you weren't here anymore? I ate the bagel!"

(*)

A Catholic priest asked, "When will you finally give up the old dietary prejudice and start eating pork?"

Geiger replied, "At your wedding, your Reverence."

🌱 🌱 🌱

On the High Holy Days, seats in the synagogue are often sold in advance, to provide revenue for synagogue upkeep. In a small *shul* in Coney Island, a Jew without a ticket came running up to the door. "Let me in, let me in! I must see Abe Baum!"

The *shammes* barred his way. "No one gets in without a ticket!"

"It's an emergency! I'll come right out! It'll only take five seconds!"

"OK," said the *shammes*. "But don't let me catch you praying!"

🌱 🌱 🌱

The visiting rabbi stopped in the middle of his sermon and signaled to the *shammes*. "In the second row," he whispered, "is a man sound asleep. Wake him up."

"That's not fair," said the *shammes*.

"What do you mean, 'not fair'?"

"You put him to sleep, you wake him up."

The Jews Already Had Diabetes

🌿 🌿 🌿

Among the best known, most oft-told of "Anglo-Saxon"-Jewish anecdotes is the following dialogue between priest and rabbi. The earliest published version which I was able to unearth appeared in a poorly printed anonymous booklet dated London, 1891.

A rabbi and a priest were discussing the material advantages of their respective ministries.

"The trouble with being a rabbi is that you are in a rut," the priest said. "From the day you are ordained to the day you die there is no hope for promotion."

"And a priest?" queried the rabbi.

"Come now, Rabbi; you know better than to say that! I can become a bishop."

"So you're a bishop. So what?"

"Why, an effective bishop could be promoted to cardinal. What do you think of that?"

"So you become a cardinal. So what?"

"My dear Rabbi, a cardinal, as you should know, could become a Pope."

"So you become a Pope. So what?"

"Good heavens," the priest cried out in exasperation, "what do you expect a man to become—God?"

"Why not?" answered the rabbi calmly. "One of our boys made it!"

🌿 🌿 🌿

The German authorities knew that some Jews, desperate for survival, were attempting to escape deportation and death by posing as Christians. To put a stop to this practice, squads of SS troopers converged on churches throughout that sick nation. One such group entered a Berlin Evangelical church while the services were in progress.

"I want to make an announcement to your congregation," said the squad leader.

The minister could only shrug helplessly.

"Fellow Germans," began the Nazi, "I am here in the interests of racial purity. We have tolerated the inferior race for far too long, and now the time has come when we must spew them out from our midst."

The Nazi glared at the congregation. "All those whose mothers and fathers were both Jews are ordered to line up outside this church—at once."

A pitiful few rose from their seats and were hustled outside.

"And now, all those whose fathers were Jews are to get outside!"

A few more white-faced people rose and left.

"Finally, all those whose mothers were Jewish, get out!"

The minister took a figurine of Jesus Christ from its niche near the pulpit. "Allow me the honor, dear Lord, of escorting you to the door!"

☙ ☙ ☙

A priest and a rabbi, longtime friends, were discussing the oddities of their respective religions.

The Jews Already Had Diabetes

"Rabbi, tell me, why do you Jews persist in wearing both a yarmulke and a hat? Isn't the hat sufficient without the skullcap?"

"Now just a moment, my friend," retorted the rabbi. "Your own cardinals and bishops wear head coverings at church services. Even your Pope wears a yarmulke."

"That, dear Rabbi, is symbolic of a roof over their heads. But you haven't answered my question."

"I'm developing my thesis." The rabbi smiled. "A cow in a stable has a roof over her head. We Jews want not only the roof that even a cow is entitled to, but a symbol of civilization as well—a ceiling!"

❧ ❧ ❧

Rabbi Stephen S. Wise, much in demand as a lecturer, was rarely seen in his own synagogue because of his many speaking engagements.

"How is it," he was once asked, "that your congregation doesn't fire you?"

"They can't, very well," said the rabbi with a merry twinkle in his eye. "They have to find me first!"

❧ ❧ ❧

A very poor widow rushed to the house of the rabbi, tearfully demanding that she see him at once. The *rebbetzn* quickly ushered her husband into the living room.

"What can I do for you, my child?" asked the rabbi.

"*Oy*, did something terrible happen to me!" she wailed.

"What's so terrible?"

"Rabbi, with my last few pennies I bought for the *kinderlach* and for myself a piece of kosher meat, but when I got home—who can explain it?—inside my bag was a strange package with, you should pardon the expression —ham!"

The rabbi nodded gravely. "That is not good."

"We have nothing else in the house to eat." The poor woman sobbed. "And no money to buy anything else."

"But what makes you so sure it's ham?"

"It *looks* like ham!" Tears coursed down the woman's cheeks.

"Madam, you are permitted to eat it," decreed the compassionate rabbi. "Take my word for it—the flanken is kosher!"

🌱 🌱 🌱

It was a cold, wintry night, and the old married couple had just gone to bed.

"Goldie, why do you keep pulling away from me like that?" he asked.

"Your feet are cold."

"That's no excuse," he said unhappily. "You didn't act like this before we were married."

🌱 🌱 🌱

"How am I doing?" the writer answered his friend.
"You have no idea how popular my writing has become.
Why, since I last saw you, my readers have doubled!"

"Well, *mazel tov!* I didn't know you got married."

🌱 🌱 🌱

A *melamed* was given to taking a little nip while his
pupils droned on. And when this became known, parents
began to withdraw their boys from his class.

His wife pleaded with him to change his ways. "Give
up drinking and you'll get the pupils back."

Sighed the *melamed,* "You tell me to stop drinking so
I should be able to teach, but I have been teaching so I
should be able to drink."

🌱 🌱 🌱

The *melamed* asked one of his young students, "Yus-
sele, do you say your prayers before each meal?"

"No, *Melamed.*"

"What? You don't pray before each meal?"

"I don't have to. My mother's a good cook."

(*Leo Rosten*)

🌱 🌱 🌱

A friend asks the rabbi, an expectant father: "Are you hoping for a boy or a girl?"

"Naturally," the rabbi answers.

🌑 🌑 🌑

"Rabbi, I need your advice; I'm desperate," cried the worried-looking little man. "I earn a very small salary—hardly enough to support my wife and eleven children. What's more, each year brings us another baby. Tell me, Rabbi, what shall I do?"

"You really want to know?" was the rabbi's terse reply. "Do nothing for a change!"

🌑 🌑 🌑

A barrel maker of Kiev who had a wry sense of humor did not believe in imposing on the Lord.

"Dear God," he prayed, "all I'm asking from You is bread to eat and clothes to wear. Nothing more. The schnapps I'll buy myself."

🌑 🌑 🌑

Harry Rosenberg bought a shiny new Studebaker, but as he was too nervous to drive, his wife, Ida, took the wheel. Ida drove masterfully, going uptown on Lexington Avenue, until they reached 102d Street, one of the steepest hills in all New York.

Immediately the Studebaker shot out from beneath them, careening wildly down the steep incline, gathering speed by the second.

"The brakes won't hold!" Ida gasped as the foot pedal went down to the floorboard. She grabbed for the emergency brake. It flopped loosely in her hand. "*Oy vey, what'll I do!*" she wailed as the car hit ninety miles per hour, completely out of control.

"Ida, for God's sake!" Harry screamed. "Hit something cheap!"

🌷 🌷 🌷

Here is a classic expression of wit well known and often repeated by the Jews of earlier decades.

Colonel Robert Ingersoll, the famed agnostic, was scheduled to lecture at the Hartford Opera House. The coming event aroused widespread interest, and Mark Twain (also an agnostic, but a compassionate man) was asked if he planned to attend.

"No," replied Twain. "I understand that Ingersoll will talk about what he thinks of Moses. But I would be far more interested in hearing what Moses thinks of Ingersoll."

(**)

🌷 🌷 🌷

Levy, the landlord, wasn't a bad-hearted fellow, but Carl, the artist, had not paid his rent in five months, and enough is enough. So he gave the tenant an ultimatum—pay up or get out!

"You don't realize what you are doing!" Carl protested. "Why, one of these days people will pass by and look at this miserable apartment and say, 'Carl, the famous painter, lived there.' "

"I got news for you," answered Levy. "If you don't pay your rent by this evening, they'll be saying it tomorrow."

(**)

❀ ❀ ❀

Two *landsleit* met in Brooklyn. "So how is it going with you, Glickman?"

"Not so good," *krechtzed* Glickman. "Last month I spent on doctors and medicines—forty-five dollars!"

"Forty-five dollars? In one month! Back in the old country you could have been sick two *years* for that kind of money!"

❀ ❀ ❀

When an El Al plane leaves New York, the pilot greets the passengers in these words: "*Sholem aleichem,* ladies and gentlemen, and welcome to El Al airlines. This is your pilot, Itzchak Levin, wishing you a happy, restful trip, which we certainly expect to have, God willing. And if by some remote chance we do run into trouble—God forbid!—do not panic, keep calm. Your life belt is under your seat. And if you must put it on, wear it in the best of health!"

❊ ❊ ❊

Someone said you can tell if a man is a Jew by how he answers the question "How are you?" If he says, "Fine!" or "Couldn't be better," he's no Jew. For Jews, by tradition, fear that boasting (of good health or good luck) may attract some jealous and punishing evil spirit. The typical Jewish reply to "How do you feel?" is "Not bad," or "So-so." If he's from Brooklyn, the reply is "How should I feel?"

Ben-Gurion Did Not Come on a White Donkey

IN a recent anecdote from Israel, the question was raised: Why did Ben-Gurion not want to be proclaimed king of the country? The answer is: Because he did not relish the idea of being called King David II.

🌸 🌸 🌸

I went into a *schenk* (saloon) in Meah Shearim, the ultra Orthodox quarter of Jerusalem. It was before the election in Israel, and I got into an argument with a fellow at the bar. He was handing out pamphlets urging the people not to vote. I finally said to him, "How do you know Ben-Gurion isn't the Messiah?" and he answered, "He didn't come on a white donkey."

🌸 🌸 🌸

During a pogrom, the wife of a rabbi was raped before his very eyes by a Cossack. Afterward she humbly begged her husband's pardon, assuring him that she was helpless and could not prevent the rape. The rabbi conceded that the rapist was stronger than she, but he asked, "But why were you shaking your behind?"

🌺 🌺 🌺

Then there is the story of the Cossack raping a Jewish woman during a pogrom. And the young daughter pleads with the Cossack, "Please leave my mother alone, she's an old woman. You can take me, but leave her alone."

The woman raised her head from the pillow and said, "Keep quiet, a pogrom is a pogrom."

🌺 🌺 🌺

A worried mother cautioned her small son, on their first visit to Disneyland: "Now I'm warning you, Mendel, hold tight to my hand. If you get lost, don't come crying to me."

🌺 🌺 🌺

Milton Rosen, a poor man all his life, was struck by a car and killed instantly. So his wife collected $3,000 from the insurance company.

But Mrs. Rosen was far from comforted. "*Oy,* what terrible luck!" she moaned. "Ever since we were married, we lived in poverty, and now that we have a little something, Milton has to go and die!"

🌷 🌷 🌷

A young rabbi was flying from New York to Los Angeles. They were 20,000 feet over the Rocky Mountains when, without warning, one of the engines fell off. The pilot, struggling with the controls, managed to bring the plane back to an even keel, and then asked the stewardess if the passengers were overly nervous.

"They're near the point of panic," she told him.

The pilot turned the controls over to the co-pilot and went back to where the rabbi was sitting. "The rest of the passengers are alarmed," he said, his voice urgent. "Do something religious."

So the rabbi took up a collection.

🌷 🌷 🌷

Jake, the coachman, once drove a great rabbi from one town to the next. This rabbi was known for his brilliance. They stopped over at an inn. When the guests at the inn saw the great rabbi was in the inn, they showed him great respect. Rabbi Teitelbaum had traveled to collect money for a very worthy cause. (If he went, it must have been worthy.) When he continued on the trip and

175

stopped in various places, the rabbi received great respect, and the poor coachman became very jealous. So the coachman asked a favor of the rabbi. "Rabbi Teitelbaum, is it possible that I might find out what it's like to receive so much honor. Would you change clothes with me so I could find out?"

"I'd be glad to, Jake, but what will happen if they question you about the Torah? How will you fool them then?"

"Trust me," answered Jake.

They changed clothes and continued their trip. Soon they arrived at an inn. Outside were many people wanting to see the great rabbi. All, of course, thought that Jake was the great scholar, and all went to greet him. They went in to sit down at the table, and they put Jake in the center, and Rabbi Teitelbaum, after all only a coachman, was stuck in a corner. Rabbi Teitelbaum however listened very carefully to what was going on. One of the guests asked Jake if he would please explain a difficult passage in one of the commentaries on the Talmud. The rabbi knew that this was difficult and wondered what the ignorant coachman would answer. Jake looked briefly at the text and then at the men around the table. "You mean to tell me that you don't understand this? Why, if you're the brightest men in town, I'm ashamed of your city. Such a question even my coachman could answer."

(*)

❧ ❧ ❧

Danile Abramovich Chwolson (1819-1910), a Jewish professor under the czars, had been converted to the

Greek Orthodox faith. When asked if he had done this out of conviction or expedience, he dryly replied, "I accepted baptism entirely out of conviction—the conviction that it is better to be a professor in the Imperial Academy in St. Petersburg than a teacher in a *cheder* in Vilna."

🌺 🌺 🌺

Little Milton's first day home from school, his mother ran out eagerly to meet him.

"So what did you learn?"

"I learned to write," said Milton.

"On the first day already you learned to write? America *gonif!* So what did you write?"

"How should I know?" said Milton. "I can't read."

(*Leo Rosten*)

🌺 🌺 🌺

Hassein Heikal, editor of the influential Cairo daily *Al Ahram*, warns his readers that the Israelis will soon be able to produce an atomic bomb.

Which reminds me of an incident involving the late Irish playwright Brendan Behan, who once told a Canadian audience: "Israel will send a couple of matzoh balls around the moon before you Canadians succeed in sending a spaceship there."

I have been assured on good authority that neither the

Egyptians nor the Canadians have any cause for worry. Israel is making no atom bomb and has no intention of sending matzoh balls around the moon. They need all the matzoh balls they can make for next Passover, with God's help.

🌱 🌱 🌱

By unfortunate coincidence four ambitious merchants opened fish markets in the same block of Seventh Avenue. All four were hurting for business, of course, and each one wracked his brain for a way to attract the customers to his own establishment. Manny finally hit upon a plan of simple advertising. He put a big sign in the window which read MANNY'S IS THE BEST FISH MARKET IN NEW YORK. Soon after, Sol decided to do him one better. He had a sign made up which read SOL'S IS THE BEST FISH MARKET IN NEW YORK STATE. It was not long before Ben joined in the competition. He had his sign maker display the slogan BEN'S IS THE BEST FISH MARKET IN THE UNITED STATES. But Louie outdid them all, and without making any extravagant claim. He simply put out a sign in his window which read LOUIE'S IS THE BEST FISH MARKET ON THIS BLOCK.

🌱 🌱 🌱

Khrushchev and Kennedy were in conference, trying to agree on the terms of the worldwide nonaggression pact. Before Khrushchev would sign he wanted Kennedy to announce to the United States that Adam and Eve were the first Communists. After the meeting was adjourned, Kennedy wrestled with the problem all through the afternoon and well into the night. In a sudden flash of inspiration he decided to call Ben-Gurion of Israel, a noted authority on matters historical and Biblical.

"What do you think, eh, Mr. Prime Minister?" Kennedy asked, after he had explained Khrushchev's demand.

"Tell him you agree entirely," said the Israeli. "Adam and Eve were Communists because they had nothing to wear, no place to go, nothing to eat but apples, and still they believed they were in paradise!"

🌷 🌷 🌷

Old man Ginsberg was a reformed sinner. When his daughter Natalie went away to college, he let a few months go by before he woke up to the idea of all the temptations on campus, all the possible occasions for wrongdoing. Then he could think of nothing else. Finally he bought a new Bible in the bookstore and took it to the post office to send his daughter. When the postal clerk asked if there was anything breakable inside the package, Ginsberg answered, "You said it! The Ten Commandments!"

🌷 🌷 🌷

From Minsk in the old country comes the story of Chozeber, the con man, who enjoyed a career as shoplifter for forty years without once getting into trouble. "I'll tell you how I do it," Chozeber recently told a persistent newspaper reporter. "With every single action I perform, I have three tests. For example, supposing I'm in the market for a hatchet. I try it on a straw. If it cuts it through, good. If it fails to cut, so what? Then I strike the blade against a hard object of metal. If sparks fly, good. If not, so what? Finally, I hide it under my coat. If the shopkeeper does not notice, good. If he does, so what? I put it back!"

❦ ❦ ❦

Heinrich Heine loved women and the theater, in that order. Once he fell madly in love with an actress who was performing as the star of the hit play of the year. Without delay, Heine positioned himself at the stage door and waited for the stunning creature to emerge after her performance. She came out, and he approached her with unfaltering self-confidence.

"Mademoiselle," said Heine, "please honor me by listening to a proposal. Would you care to be escorted to your home by a talented, wealthy, handsome, young aristocrat?"

The ingenue smiled and shook her head. "Without offense, monsieur, but I would definitely prefer not to be so escorted." And she began to walk up the lane to where her coachman was waiting.

But Heine stepped around her and blocked her way.

"Then permit me to offer myself as a candidate for the honor. For I am neither handsome, wealthy, nor aristocratic, and you can see for yourself that I am no longer young. The fact is, I am poor, a bit weather-beaten, and a poet. My name is Heinrich Heine." With that, he offered the beautiful actress his arm, which she took, and together they strolled up the lane to her carriage.

❧ ❧ ❧

Jack Lehvine was griping to his partner over lunch at the club. "My wife Muriel is driving me *meshuggeh*," he complained. "Every week she wants more money. Last week it was two hundred fifty. The week before one twenty-five. And this morning she comes up to me while I'm shaving and says she's got to have four of the big ones. Honest to God, I'll have an ulcer with her before I'm through."

The partner was sympathetic, but curious, too. "But, Jack," he said, "what in the world does Muriel *do* with all that money you give her?"

At this, Jack grinned. "Who said I gave her anything? I just can't stand her asking!"

❧ ❧ ❧

Back in Odessa in the old days Zachariah, the tinker, was past his prime. He was, in fact, growing old and a bit feeble. During the Feast of Tabernacles Zachariah built his hut or *succah* as usual, to dwell in for seven days as all devout Jews should do during this holiday. Only this year he went wandering about the village with his boards and canvas and hammer and built his hut by mistake on the property of an influential bureaucrat, a member of the village council and a Gentile. On the very same day that this fellow discovered Zachariah's unsightly hut on his property, he had the old man summoned to court and tried before the judge. The judge listened to the testimony on both sides and then rendered the verdict: "Complaint sustained. Zachariah, the tinker, must remove his tabernacle from defendant's property, and he must do so within the next thirty days."

Berman, an American spy, was ordered by the Central Intelligence Agency to cross over the Iron Curtain and make contact with another CIA spy named Shapiro. The password with which they would identify each other was: "The sun is shining."

Under the dark of the moon, a U.S. Air Force plane dropped Berman by parachute into the woods on the outskirts of Moscow. Our hero buried the parachute, as he had been instructed, and then skulked into the city, keeping to the shadows and moving stealthily as befits a high-class espionage agent.

He had memorized Shapiro's address, but when he reached the place, he found, to his chagrin, that it was a four-story apartment building. A resourceful fellow, Berman consulted the letterboxes in the hallway, where he found not one but two Shapiros listed. So he tried ringing the doorbell of the first one.

When the occupant opened the door Berman asked, "Are you Shapiro?"

"Yes, I am," said the man.

"All right, the sun is shining," said the American agent, giving the password.

"Oh, no!" the other said. "I'm Shapiro, the butcher. You want Shapiro, the spy—he's on the third floor!"

🌷 🌷 🌷

Cohen, the beggar, is trying to take a nap. The nearby play of children disturbs him.

"Why are you wasting your time here," asks Cohen, "when on the other side of town Shapiro is handing out free apples?"

The children run to claim the fruit.

Cohen goes back to his rest but rises with a start and asks himself, "Why am *I* wasting my time sleeping when Shapiro is handing out free apples?"

🌷 🌷 🌷

I heard this one in Israel on my last visit: The Arab chieftain with ten oil wells and thirty wives was driving along the desert road in his big Cadillac. Off in the distance he saw a young fifteen-year-old Arab girl, who struck his fancy. He called her over, patted her on the head, and said, "Little girl, would you join my harem?" and the little girl answered, "I can't, Papa, I can't."

🕎 🕎 🕎

A cable from Anwar el-Sadat to Alexei Kosygin in the Kremlin: "Israelis advance on Cairo, send help immediately."

No response from the Kremlin.

Another cable from Sadat to Kosygin: "Israelis have entered Cairo, and they are raping our women."

This time a reply did come. It said: *"Mazel tov. Twenty years from now you'll have a good army."*

🕎 🕎 🕎

Native-born Israelis pride themselves on the use of pure Hebrew. Yiddish, being the most immediate rival, is held in some contempt. In fact, a few years ago if you approached a sabra and asked directions in Yiddish, you were ignored. This situation sometimes created peculiar dilemmas, as in the case of the Jewish tourist from New York who went swimming at the beach in Tel Aviv and suddenly found himself being swept out to sea. In Yiddish he cried, *"Helft, ratevet! Ich kan nisht reden kein Hebreish."* Which translates: "Help, save me! I can't speak Hebrew!"

🕎 🕎 🕎

During the sixteenth century the King of Portugal signed a decree specifying that all Jews had to wear a particular kind of cap whenever they ventured out of doors. The archbishop and members of the King's Cabinet were summoned to witness the royal signature. But as the King raised his pen to apply it to the decree, his Prime Minister extracted three of the Jewish caps from his pocket.

"What are those caps for?" the King's steward demanded.

"One is for me," said the Prime Minister. "I looked up my genealogy and found that some of my ancestors were of a distinguished Jewish family. Another is for the archbishop, who, whether he knows it or not, is also descended from Jews. And the third cap is for His Majesty, who according to the venerable records, belongs in the same category."

❦ ❦ ❦

Under the czars a good many Jews sneaked into Russia's big industrial cities and procured work under assumed Russian names, keeping as best they could their affiliation with Judaism a secret. High holidays, however, represented a real problem. The undercover Levys, Cohens, and Steinbergs would suffer torments, wondering if the factory foreman would put two and two together when he noticed ten or fifteen new employees absent on Yom Kippur.

One year, so the story is told, an old-time foreman and true patriotic Russian actually invaded the nearby synagogue on Yom Kippur and discovered the new men he had hired deeply immersed in prayer. The foreman looked around once, then returned to the door of the synagogue and opened it a crack, peering up and down the street as if to check on who was watching. Then hurriedly he returned inside, donned a *kittel*, wrapped himself in a *tallis*, and plunged into the service as devoutly as the rest.

🌺 🌺 🌺

Once long ago, an Islamic prince living in southern Spain employed a Jewish funny man to divert him during the idle hours of the long summer days. The prince asked his jester to make him a list of foolish and stupid acts performed by members of the court.

A week or so passed, and the prince wanted to know, "Is my name on your list?"

The jester held up a scroll for inspection and replied, "Indeed it is, oh, noble prince!" Then the Moor grew angry and demanded an explanation. "Ten days ago," said the jester, "you gave five thousand pieces of gold to a Turkish merchant who promised to bring you a rope of pearls." True enough, admitted the prince. "How do you know he will return with the pearls?" the jester asked.

"That Turk is an honest man!" thundered the prince. "He will come within a fortnight, fulfilling his share of the bargain. And what will you say then, jester?"

Without hesitation the jester replied, "If he does, then I'll remove your name from the list and put his on!"

Ben-Gurion Did Not Come on a White Donkey

❀ ❀ ❀

Tamar, the widow of the late great rabbi David de Sola Pool, one evening told her husband that she had just heard a professor say that it was the Arabs who wrote the Ten Commandments. And the rabbi said, "Yes? Well, let them *keep* them."

❀ ❀ ❀

Toastmaster George Jessel listened attentively as the chairman at an Israel Bonds banquet described, in eloquent terms, the Holy Land's accomplishments in cultivating arid areas.

"For the first time since the Creation," explained the chairman, "apples are growing in many territories of the country."

Jessel, apparently, did not agree with the statement. When it came his time to speak, he asked, "Who says they never had apples? What did Adam bite into—a dill pickle?"

(**)

❀ ❀ ❀

Two Israeli spies, caught in Cairo, were put up against the wall. The firing squad marched in. The Egyptian captain asked the first spy, "Do you have any last wish?"

"A cigarette."

The captain gave him a cigarette, lighted it, and asked the second spy, "Do you have a last request?"

Without a word, the second spy spit in the captain's face.

"Harry!" cried the first spy. "Please! Don't make trouble."

🌱 🌱 🌱

In France, an elderly Jew, tired of hearing a young man boast of his ancestry, finally said, "Listen, La Fontaine; I knew your grandfather, who changed his name to La Fontaine from Schpritzwasser [Squirtwater]. And he told me that *his* father changed his name to Schpritzwasser from what everyone called him, which was Moishe the *Pisher!* So please, don't put on airs, 'La Fontaine.' "

(Leo Rosten)

🌱 🌱 🌱

Milton Berle, "Mr. Television," was speaking at a Zionist banquet.

"While I was in Israel," he told the assembled guests, "they asked me if I would like to visit the tomb of Israel's unknown soldier. I said I would, and an escort picked me up in a limousine.

"When I arrived at the tomb I couldn't believe my

eyes. There in big letters, was inscribed, 'Here lies Israel's unknown soldier, Hyman Goldfarb, Furrier.'

" 'But I thought this was the tomb of an unknown soldier! How can he possibly have a name?' "

" 'As a soldier,' they assured me, 'he was certainly unknown, but as a furrier, he was famous!' "

＊ ＊ ＊

DOCTOR: Private Ginsberg, is there any medical reason why you should not be inducted into the army?
DRAFTEE: Believe me, Doctor, half my insides are missing!
DOCTOR: What's your internal problem?
DRAFTEE: No guts!

＊ ＊ ＊

I took a taxi in Jerusalem for Haifa, a drive of about two and a half hours. The taxi driver was a man in his mid-fifties. His name was Bazalel Katz, and we had a long, extended conversation.

Mr. Katz told me he was born in Germany. His parents were Orthodox. And because of his name, other boys made fun of him. He grew to hate the name Bazalel. He begged his father to let him change it. He even had another name picked out—Heinz. But his father said, "Your grandfather was Bazalel, and you will remain Bazalel. You will not change your name while I am alive."

When Hitler became Chancellor, the Katz family moved to Vienna. The young man's name still caused him discomfort. "How do you spell it?" they'd ask. "What kind of name is that? What does it mean—Bazalel —and how do you pronounce it?" His name tortured him all over the continent of Europe.

Then he came to Israel in 1938. At the port of entry the immigration inspector asked his name. "Bazalel Katz," he replied.

My taxi driver said the immigration inspector kept right on writing. "Can you imagine that?" he said. "The inspector didn't even look up. He just wrote the name. I was home."

� � �

A young student prided himself on his ability to confuse the wisest of scholars. Once, when he was surrounded by friends, he sought to prove his self-asserted cleverness, so he asked the town sage, "What was the first thing Eve did when Adam came home late one night?"

"She counted his ribs," said the sage promptly.

� � �

Speaking of bishops, the comedian Joey Bishop was asked why his father, a rabbi, had not changed his name, as had the son.

"He was quite right to keep his Jewish name," said Joey. "After all, how would it sound to address him as Rabbi Bishop?"

❀ ❀ ❀

A Russian Jew was arrested by the Soviet secret police when they found American matches in his possession.

When his trial came up, he told the judge, "Your Honor, it is true that I was using capitalistic matches, but only to light our people's matches."

Noodnik the Fenster-Mender

NOT since the days of the Norse sagas has there appeared a hero of the stature of Noodnik the Fenster-Mender, who was a legend in his own time on two sides of the Atlantic Ocean. Noodnik once wrote to the Postmaster General to complain about the filthy smut advertisements that were being mailed to his home, and what's more, he sent off $10 for one of the books and they never sent it! On another day he went to the fancy funeral of his boss, who had suffered a coronary while on vacation in Florida, and remarked to one of the relatives: "Doesn't the old man look wonderful! Those two weeks in Palm Beach did him a world of good!" Noodnik, if not exactly proper material for an epic, was at least fit for an *epis*.

Back in the old country, he was ambling along the streets of Moscow late one night when he was stopped by a palace guard. "Your passport!" the officer demanded. "What do you need with my passport," Noodnik replied, "when you have me here in person?"

On another occasion, Noodnik was walking down the Nevsky Plaza when a big, burly stranger walked up to him, punched him in the side of the head, and knocked him to the ground. "There, Ezra the Tool-Maker, take that. And let it be a lesson for the future." Dazed, Noodnik sat up and began to laugh. "Ha-ha," he said, "the joke's on you. I'm not Ezra the Tool-Maker. I'm Noodnik the Fenster-Mender!"

On still another fine day Noodnik dropped by the establishment of his best friend, who ran an antique shop. Noodnik pushed open the front door of the shop, poked his head in, and hollered, "Hello. What's new?"

Noodnik's parents wanted to send him to medical college—not to study, but to be studied. However, Noodnik decided he wanted to come to America. On the way over, his son complained, "I'm sorry, Father, but I don't want to go to America." Said Noodnik, "Shut up and keep swimming."

When Noodnik applied for his first job in the New World, the foreman asked him where he had last been employed and for how long. "I worked in the fenster-mender shop in Kiev," said Noodnik, "for forty years." The foreman was skeptical. "How old are you, buddy?" he asked. "Thirty-seven," said Noodnik. "But you see, I put in a lot of overtime."

Noodnik was forced to look elsewhere for a job and eventually wound up street peddling, like so many others of his generation. Once, as evening drew on, Noodnik had suffered a particularly disappointing day. Not a single sale, not a cent of profit, not even a person to talk to from dawn to dusk! As he was sitting on the curbstone contemplating the best method of suicide, an old lady came up to his pushcart and began picking over the assorted merchandise. At last she extracted a cotton shawl, which she felt with her fingertips for ten minutes, held up to the fading light, and finally wrapped around her

shoulder. "How much?" the elderly woman asked. Noodnik's heart was beating wildly. "What would you say to
one penny?" Noodnik replied. "Sorry," said the old lady,
taking off the shawl and replacing it among the other
items on the pushcart. "Not interested." And she started
down the street. "Wait!" called Noodnik, seizing her by
her arm. "At least make me an offer!"

These were difficult times for Noodnik and his family—
so difficult in fact that Noodnik lost his superb sense of
balance and contemplated converting to Christianity.
The almost irresistible inducement—to a man in Noodnik's situation—was an offer advertised on the façade of a
church in the neighborhood which read: *"One hundred
dollars cash to any man who joins this church today!"*
Gulping, closing his eyes, and making fists, Noodnik entered, talked to the minister for a few minutes, and
signed the register. That evening at the supper table
Noodnik proudly waved a bunch of limp tens and fives
under the noses of his loved ones. His wife promptly took
half of his conversion money to pay the landlord overdue
rent. Uncle Bendle got another twenty to buy a hearing
aid. Aaron wanted $25 for a set of secondhand golf clubs.
After supper Noodnik sat staring dazedly at the remaining
five-dollar bill. "It never fails," he muttered to himself.
"As soon as these Jews run into a Gentile with a little
money, they rob him blind!"

Early next morning Noodnik went over to see his
bookie friend Morris Levy. "Morris," Noodnik pleaded,
"you've got to help me! I want you should convert to
Christianity as soon as possible—today even!" Morris
stared wide-eyed. "You're *meshuggeh*, Noodnik! Why
would I want to do a thing like that?" Tears came to

Noodnik's eyes. "For my sake, Morris. I've got to have at least one Christian friend!" With a reluctant "All right, already," Morris Levy accompanied Noodnik to the church to be baptized. "It is the custom," the minister informed them, "to take a new name on the occasion of Christian baptism. Have you picked out a name?" The holy man looked searchingly from Morris to Noodnik. The two new converts called time out for a brief whispered conference. "Reb Minister," Noodnik said at last, "we have decided to have my friend Morris Levy christened Martin Luther." The minister beamed. "An excellent choice and an illustrious antecedent," he said. "But may I inquire the reason for your choice?" Noodnik and Morris exchanged glances. "Certainly," said the latter. "It's so I won't have to change the initials on my shirts."

Next, Noodnik had to receive communion. He was told that he had to fast from midnight Saturday before taking the wafer during Sunday services. Early Sunday morning Noodnik showed up at the church before the commencement of services. He sought out the minister. "Please, Reb Minister, make an exception! I'm dying of thirst. Could I have just a sip of seltzer before receiving communion?" The minister pondered. "Seltzer I haven't got handy. But you've been such a dutiful convert that a little glass water wouldn't hurt." And so the good man poured Noodnik a glass of water. "Such kindness!" Noodnik exclaimed as he greedily downed the water. "Next Sunday I won't even eat pickled herring for breakfast!"

Prosperity came to Noodnik in an unexpected way. One evening he was crossing the street to go home and was struck down by a slow-moving auto. Noodnik played dead and was taken to the hospital. "I'm completely and totally paralyzed from the waist down," he told the doctors, nurses, and insurance investigators. That night Noodnik stopped a tall majestic-looking nurse who was hurrying down the corridor outside his room. "Nurse," said Noodnik. "Please bring a hot-water bottle. My toes are cold as ice." The nurse acted insulted. "Mister," she said, "you've asked the wrong person. I happen to be the head nurse." Said Noodnik, "Pish-posh, so send me the foot nurse."

Noodnik's case finally came to trial, and he testified from a wheelchair. "When did you first realize that you were suffering from paralysis?" asked the attorney for the insurance company. Noodnik's lawyer jumped to his feet. "I object, your honor!" Noodnik quieted him with a wave of the hand. "Let him ask. I want to answer." The other attorney repeated the question. "You don't have to answer! Objection!" shouted Noodnik's lawyer, unable to restrain himself. Now the judge intervened. "If the defendent wishes to answer, I see no reason to sustain the objection. Please proceed with the questioning, Counsellor." Once again the other attorney faced Noodnik. "When did you first realize you were suffering from paralysis?" he repeated. "I don't remember," replied Noodnik.

A few days later Noodnik lay in his hospital bed awaiting the decision on his case. The telephone by his bedside rang, and Noodnik picked it up. His lawyer was jubilant. "Justice has triumphed!" he told Noodnik. "Really?" responded Noodnik. "So when do we start our first appeal?"

Later the lawyer came over to see Noodnik for a conference. "You won the decision, and the judge awarded you fifty thousand dollars!" the attorney said. "But actually, I'm not so sure it's a good deal for you. The agents for that insurance company are noted for their vigilance. They'll watch you like a hawk for the next fifty years. If you get out of bed or step out of the wheelchair, they'll have you back in court on charges of perjury and fraud." Noodnik smiled indulgently, as if to forgive his lawyer's innocence. "You think I'm not prepared for all that?" said Noodnik. "Why do you think I have an ambulance waiting to take me to the airport, and why do you think I have reservations for an afternoon flight to France?" The lawyer shook his head emphatically. "You won't get away with it," he said. "They have agents in Paris, too, you know." Noodnik's eyebrows went up. "Paris? Who said anything about Paris? I'm going to Lourdes, and then hoo-boy! are you going to see a miracle take place!"

On the flight home from Lourdes, Noodnik was completely recovered from his paralysis. But the air pressure in the plane gave him trouble in the eardrums. "Stewardess!" Noodnik complained. "It's the ears. They're closing up on me or something." The girl brought him a package of Chiclets. "These ought to help," she said cheerfully. When they landed in New York, Noodnik thanked the stewardess as he walked out the exit door. "Just one thing," he said. "When can I take the chewing gum out of my ears?"

Now Noodnik was affluent, and the first thing he did was open a shiny new fenster-mender shop, a cross between Dubrow's and the Guggenheim Museum. The very first week an old assistant Noodnik had hired, mostly out of kindness, approached the boss and said, "Sir, tomorrow my wife, Ruth, and I celebrate our fiftieth wedding anniversary. I was hoping you would give me the day off."

Noodnik thought it over. "Well, all right," he said reluctantly. "But I hope I won't have to put up with this special favor business every fifty years!"

A short time later Noodnik made an important decision: He turned in his crucifix and returned to the faith of his fathers. One day at the office a sour-looking solicitor came by and asked Noodnik for a donation to support the work of the Sisters of Mercy in the Philippines. Business wasn't no good, so Noodnik had to refuse. "That's the trouble with you Jews," said the sour-looking man. "You only contribute to Jewish organizations." Noodnik thought this was unjust and told the man so. "Distinctions I don't make when I give to charity," he said. "And as often as not, my donations go to organizations which are strictly Gentile. Why, just last week I wrote a check to the Mental Health Institute!"

Noodnik bought his wife a new mink coat, but his son Aaron was on a conservation kick and complained. "Think about the poor animal, Mama, and how he must have suffered!" His mother was shocked. "Why, Aaron!" she exclaimed. "Is that any way to talk about your father!"

Years earlier, when Aaron was six, his mother had taken him for a walk through an uptown residential district. Two very respectable middle-aged ladies were just coming out of afternoon church services and bumped into Aaron. As they went about their way, one turned to the other and said, "Louisa, did you notice that little boy?" Louisa linked arms with her friend and replied, "Indeed I did, Abigail, and my heart went out to him." Abigail slowed her pace. "It certainly seems a shame. But I don't think we could be mistaken about a thing like that." Louisa agreed. "Oh, he's Jewish, all right. It's written all over his face." Both ladies sighed. "And him so young!" said Abigail, as they resumed their stroll.

When Aaron's Bar Mitzvah rolled around, Noodnik spared no expense. Never was seen such food! Never did the twin cantors perform more ably! And the decorations! They were beyond compare. On the corner of the table stood a magnificent life-sized statue of a Bar Mitzvah boy carved out of halvah. One of the jealous relatives sought out Noodnik and asked sarcastically, "Who carved your statue, Epstein or Lipschitz?" Noodnik was equal to the jibe. "Why, it was Epstein, of course. Lipschitz works only in chopped chicken liver!"

Noodnik's wife, Simonetta, worked in a dairy restaurant on Second Avenue, and everyone was much grieved when she took ill and lay dying of a fatal disease. The rabbi recited the prayer for forgiveness and even read from the Book of Psalms. Nothing helped. Finally, he called all the relatives into the sickroom and explained the situation. "If everyone here will donate a portion of his own life, maybe God will understand how much we value the good health and continued existence of this dear woman," he told them. "I would gladly give two weeks of my own life that Mama might live," said little Aaron. "I will donate a month of my life—for her sake," said Uncle Bendel. "I will give six months," said Aunt Reba gallantly, her lips quivering. "Pikers!" snorted Noodnik contemptuously. "I will gladly donate twenty years"—they all gasped in admiration—"of my brother-in-law's life."

But none of these noble last-minute efforts were effective, and soon it was apparent to the most optimistic among the mourners at the bedside that they had better start making plans for the funeral. "Uncle Mendel had six hired cars for *his* funeral," said little Aaron. "Yes, Aaron," said Aunt Reba, "but he could afford it with no trouble. We'd better not overdo it, you know. Two cars will be plenty." Noodnik thought about it in the heavy moment of silence that followed. "What do we need two cars for?" he finally announced. "Isn't that wasteful? Can't we all fit in one car? Or maybe one of those big taxis with the seats that fold out?" With that, Simonetta opened her eyes and moaned, "If you cheapskates will hand me my clothes, I'll get up and walk to the cemetery."

Two days later, it was all over. Noodnik and his boy returned from the graveyard in Long Island and tried to adjust to the silent, seemingly empty house. Noodnik comforted himself with a belief in spiritualism, and every night for a month he tried to make contact with the departed spirit of his beloved wife. All to no avail. Then late one night, he had an inspiration. The dairy restaurant on Second Avenue! That was where she had spent most of her time the past several years. And that was the logical place where Noodnik was most likely to make contact with her. And so he and Aaron went to the restaurant and sat at one of the tables until the place closed and got special permission from the manager to stay after closing time so that there would be no interference or distractions. Around one o'clock in the morning, Noodnik heard a familiar voice speaking to him out of the air, "Noodnik, is that you and Aaron?"

"Yes, darling wife. It's us," was the reply. "Is your spirit at rest where you are now?"

"Noodnik," said the voice, "my ectoplasm isn't material enough to hear you plainly. You'll have to speak up."

"Come closer, darling wife. Come stand by us and let us feel your closeness."

"I can't do that, Noodnik, and you know it. That table you're sitting at is out of my station!"

A year passed and Noodnik's heart healed. In fact, he began thinking about acquiring a new wife. He went to the *shadchan* and whispered in his ear: "A young one." The next night Noodnik went to the office of the *shadchan* and was introduced to an attractive young Jewish girl from the Bronx. "Where have you been all my life?" he asked for openers. "Well," said the obviously disgruntled maiden, "for the first forty years of it, I wasn't even born yet!"

The next day Noodnik returned to the *shadchan* and said that he would settle for "something more my style." So that night Noodnik returned to the office, and the creature to whom he was introduced put him in a rage. He excused himself and dragged the *shadchan* over to a corner. "You fraud! You swindler!" Noodnik whispered. "How dare you insult me like this! Why, that female is twenty years older than I am, and she's got a face that would stop a clock. She has one leg only, and her front teeth are missing! Her clothes are old and shabby. She's dyed her hair purple, and you can tell by the way she squints that she wears glasses, only has left them off to make a good impression. This is an outrage!" The *shadchan* apologized, saying that she was the only female available on such short notice, and that she wasn't as bad as Noodnik had painted her. "Oh, and incidentally," the professional man added, "you don't have to whisper. On top of everything else, she's deaf."

SAYINGS OF NOODNIK THE FENSTER-MENDER:

A man is young if a lady can make him miserable.
A man is young if a lady can make him glad.

A man is middle-aged if a lady can make him glad, but can no longer make him miserable. But a man is old, very old, if a lady can make him neither.

When a wise man goes looking for a new bride, he should take with him an ignoramus as an expert.

A rich man's daughter is always beautiful.

You haven't really lived until you have died in California!

Jews who can't make good in the clothing business dream of becoming disc jockeys.

A man who is very smart everyone says is lucky.

The best thing that can happen to anyone is not to be born in the first place. But to how many of us does this happen? Not one person in millions and millions!

Me is the objectionable case of I!

My definition of a year is a period of three hundred and sixty-five disappointments.

Never Marry a Shikse

RABBI FRANKEL was young, progressive, and very much oriented in the direction of social problems. Of the many invitations he received to do volunteer work, one consisted of a visit to a mental hospital, where the rabbi was to give a little talk to the ward occupied by the hopelessly insane. Before he began, the rabbi was warned by the psychiatric attendant that some of the patients might interrupt his address with meaningless shouts or cries; the rabbi would do well to ignore everything he heard and proceed with his speech.

After approximately twenty minutes of sermonizing, one of the patients jumped up and screamed, "I can't stand it! You are without a doubt the most boring and asinine speaker we have ever had in this ward!" With that, the distracted fellow ran down the corridor and disappeared into the recreation parlor.

Rabbi Frankel was shaken, but he managed to conclude his address. At that point he was approached once again by the psychiatric aide, who was beaming with pleasure. "Rabbi," said the attendant, "you have accomplished a miracle and done this hospital a great service. You know that fellow who spoke up during your speech?

Well, that's the first rational statement he's made in five years!"

❀ ❀ ❀

When Rabbi Klein announced that he was planning to resign, the congregation was deeply concerned. They sent a spokesman to express their fears and regrets to the departing rabbi. "Don't worry," said Rabbi Klein. "I am going to appoint a successor who will be a better man than I was."

But the spokesman was not cheered at all by this information. "That's what worries us," he said. "The last rabbi told us the same thing."

❀ ❀ ❀

When a rich garment manufacturer died and went to the Great Garment Center in the sky, his family grieved openly and wondered who among them would get what out of the estate. A few weeks following the funeral, the old man's attorney relieved their anxiety forever. "Being of sound mind," he read from the will to the assembled *mishpocheh* (family), "I spent all my money on pretty girls before I died."

❀ ❀ ❀

On one of the many occasions in recent years when the air-raid alarm sounded over the roofs of Tel Aviv, Hymie, the tailor, lingered in the upstairs bedroom.

"Come down, Hymie, hurry!" cried his wife from the basement shelter. "What are you doing up there at a time like this?"

Hymie shouted down, "I'm looking for my teeth."

And the wife shouted back, "Never mind your teeth, Hymie! What do you think they're dropping on us—chicken sandwiches?"

🌷 🌷 🌷

Israeli soldiers had been fighting in the Negev for weeks and holding their own against the enemy very nicely. The brave warriors' biggest hardship seemed to be chow time, for somehow the mess sergeant always managed to include a sizable amount of sand in each stew. When the men finally complained to the captain, the officer told them sternly, "The cook's job is to feed the soldiers. Your job is to fight for your country. Enough said." But one of the enlisted men could not resist adding one more point to the argument. "I don't mind fighting for my country," he said, "but do I have to eat it too?"

🌷 🌷 🌷

Ginsberg was a bachelor, and he craved fellowship and company virtually every day of his life. After much experimentation, he hit upon an almost foolproof method for attracting drinking and dining companions. He would enter a restaurant in the late-afternoon hours and order two or three pitchers of beer and a dozen or so beer mugs. Motioning to the fellows at the bar to join him, Ginsberg would adjourn to a long table and start pouring. "When Ginsberg drinks, everybody drinks!" he would announce to all within earshot. Soon he would be surrounded by jolly hangers-on, and when the beer was gone, Ginsberg would order trays of sliced salami, pickled herring, steaming *latkes,* and imported cheese. "When Ginsberg eats, everybody eats!" he would laugh, and they would all fall to with gusto. Meanwhile Ginsberg had quietly informed the manager to put everything on separate checks. When the last *latke* was consumed and everyone was sitting back glowing, Ginsberg would walk rapidly up to the cashier, leave a dollar or two at the cash register, and call back to the table of merrymakers, "When Ginsberg pays, everybody pays!" Then he would vanish out the front door.

❁ ❁ ❁

Conductor of the Berlin Symphony Orchestra, Gustav Mahler was for years the target of the anti-Semitic press, which never lost an opportunity to comment on his prominent nose. Eventually the conductor got fed up and accepted a position with the Vienna Symphony. Only when it was too late did the Berliners realize what they had lost, as they suffered through a season of inferior conducting done by Mahler's replacement. A dozen or more highly placed patrons of the Berlin Symphony wrote to Mahler asking him to return at a generous increase. "Conditions are better here at this time," they assured him. "The anti-Semite problem has dwindled."

Mahler wrote back, "Conditions may have changed, but my face remains the same. The problem may have grown smaller, but my nose has not." And he remained with the more respectful Viennese.

🌿 🌿 🌿

An Orthodox rabbi who had led an active and varied religious life in Europe wound up in his declining years at the only congregation where he could find a position— a Reform temple in one of the poorest sections of Brooklyn. A month at this job was all he could take. For his farewell address the rabbi told the congregation, "In the old country, first I was a rabbi in Yekaterinoslav. There, I found Jews but no money. Then I moved and became a rabbi in Berlin. There I found plenty of money but no Jews. Now in this congregation comes the climax of my career, for here there is no money and no Jews either!"

🌿 🌿 🌿

Moses and Franklin Delano Roosevelt were sitting on a cloud up in heaven, and Moses was teasing FDR. "Look down there now, Franklin, he-he, and see what the world is doing to your Four Freedoms." FDR took a look and then chided back in his well-known drawl, "Well, my friend, your Ten Commandments haven't fared any better."

🌷 🌷 🌷

When Walter Kaufman was a drama critic, he summed up his reaction to one New York opening by saying of the play, "I was underwhelmed."

🌷 🌷 🌷

The German Jewish poet Heinrich Heine was once reading in the public library. Two elderly ladies sat at an adjacent table chattering and gossiping for more than an hour. Heine, wishing to put down the disturbance without unduly injuring the ladies' feelings, leaned over and asked, "Excuse me, ladies, but does my reading interfere with your conversation?"

🌷 🌷 🌷

One Christmas in New York City, Mrs. Pomerantz took little Irving on a shopping trip through a bustling downtown/department store. When they arrived at the toy department, Irving dutifully waited his turn to talk

to Santa Claus, who greeted him with a cheery ho-ho-ho
and the inevitable question: "Do you believe in Santa
Claus, sonny?"

"No, I don't," snarled Irving.

Undaunted, Santa went on smiling and said, "Well,
then, do you believe in Christmas?"

"No, I sure don't," said Irving with emphasis.

Taken aback, Santa cried, "Well, what do you believe
in?"

"I believe in Chanukah," said Irving.

"Oy, a gesunt af dein kepele!" * beamed the kosher
Santa, patting Irving on the head and shoving him down
the line.

🌱　🌱　🌱

Sam Gervitz had settled in Hartford and within a few
years was thoroughly assimilated into New England manners and mores. Every Christmas Sam and his wife had a
Christmas tree with lights shining in the window and
packages spread on the floor sprinkled with snowflakes
purchased in the supermarket. When Sam's son was six,
the Gervitz family was taking a drive around town, stopping to admire the Christmas decorations in the store
windows and residences in the better neighborhoods. A
problematic look of growing perplexity strained the face
of Sam's son as the trip progressed. Finally the boy could
stand it no longer. "Tell me, Daddy," he almost ex-
ploded. "Do Gentiles believe in Christmas, just as we
do?"

---

* God bless your dear head.

Tony Curtis and Piper Laurie started their film careers around the same time, and it so happened that during the early years they were often featured in Arabian Nights adventure movies. When they finished filming one entitled *The Princess and the Thief,* they fired off a letter to their producer suggesting that he advertise the movie in New York as *The Maydel and the Gonif,* co-starring Bernie Schwartz and Rose Jacobs—which happen to be the real names of Tony Curtis and Piper Laurie.

❦ ❦ ❦

Moish and Shirley were puzzled. They had been married six years, and still no little ones had come along to add to their happiness. Finally, in desperation, Moish went to a physician to seek an answer to the problem. When the doctor asked Moish about his sexual frequency with Shirley, Moish had to confess he didn't know what the doctor was talking about. The medic concealed his amusement at Moish's naïveté but went ahead and patiently explained exactly what was involved and what was required. "But that sounds like a peculiar and highly unnatural thing to do," said Moish. "Shirley will never consent to anything like that." But the doctor reassured him. "You have my word that every normal married couple the world over performs this act when they desire to have children."

That night Moish, still dubious, approached Shirley with the information he had acquired at the doctor's office. Shirley of course was reluctant, but Moish repeated what the doctor had said, that every normal couple in the world did it.

"Are you sure he said that?" Shirley asked.

"Positive," said Moish and proceeded along the lines specified by the doctor.

A half hour later Shirley was lying in bed beaming, with Moish at her side. "You say the whole world does it?" she wanted to know again.

"Absolutely," Moish answered.

"Well, if you ask me," Shirley retorted, "it's too good for the *goyim.*"

♕ ♕ ♕

Benny's father, an Orthodox Jew, was aghast. Here was his son Benny, standing before him and saying that he was about to take a Gentile girl as a bride. "But she's going to convert," Benny wheedled. "She's studying every day with Rabbi Gitlin."

The old man was not reconciled. "A Jewish boy should marry a Jewish girl, and that's all there is to it," he grumbled.

A month later Benny paid his father a visit and complained bitterly. "Oh, why didn't I listen to you," he told the old man.

"Why, what's the matter?" his father asked.

"Well, it's Sheila," Benny explained. "For the past three Saturdays I've wanted to go down to the shop and earn some overtime. But she insists that I stay home. Rabbi Cohen told her that good Jews always keep the Sabbath. So that means no work for me on Saturdays— ever."

Benny wrung his hands and sat by his father in silence. A deep gloom descended on both. Finally the old man looked up and said, "It's like I told you. A Jewish boy's got no business marrying a *shikse*."

🌸 🌸 🌸

Schmuel Levy and Schmulke Rabinowitz opened a shop called Levy & Rabinowitz. After several years the business prospered, and Schmuel was asked to sit on the City Council, while Schmulke was regularly invited to address the Junior Chamber of Commerce. The idea hit Schmuel first. He thought, *I've got a new and different image now from when I was an immigrant's boy. I'll get me a new name.* So he went downtown and filed papers to have his name changed to Ryan. Now the company was known as Ryan and Rabinowitz.

But Schmulke was not to be outdone. He liked the idea of fitting in with his newfound friends at the Junior Chamber, and besides, Rabinowitz was a long name, and always he had to spell it out to people he didn't know. So he took the plunge and changed to Ryan. The firm was now known as Ryan and Ryan.

On the first day of operation under the new title, the phone calls began to come in for "Mr. Ryan." The switchboard operator immediately adjusted to the situa-

tion. "Which Ryan do you want?" she asked each caller.
"Levy or Rabinowitz?"

🌸 🌸 🌸

The Jews' trouble in mastering the English language is
well known, both to the struggling immigrant himself
and to the vaudeville audiences who laughed at his blun-
ders. A whole minor genre of literature grew up around
the subject—led by Anzia Yezierska and Leonard Q.
Ross (Leo Rosten). At the same time most of the humor
comes from an outlook and an attitude, rather than mere
language habits. The newcomer Jew to any nation
plunges in, muddles through, and conducts himself at all
times with confidence, as when the Jewish high school
student had to decline the Latin verb "to love" and proceeded thus: *"Amo, amas, amat, a mamus, a tatus, a
kindt."*

🌸 🌸 🌸

Abraham Birnbaum had worked many years for a Bos-
ton manufacturer with no quarrel on the side of manager
or employee. Then one year a new boss took over, a man
with a touch of anti-Semitism. He called Abe into the
office without delay. "I'm sorry," said the manager. "You
understand I have nothing against you personally. But
we have a new policy now, and all Jews must be dis-

charged immediately and excluded from employment here in the future."

"Oh, is that so?" said Abe. "Well, *ich hoff az du wist einnemen a miessa meshuna* [which is Yiddish for I hope you will die an unnatural death]!" And mustering what dignity he could, Abe strode out of the office.

That night the new manager told his wife about the incident and repeated Abe's parting words, which of course he did not understand. "There's that Jewish peddler who comes around from time to time," he remarked to his wife. "Next time you can see him, ask him what a *miessa meshuna* is." Which is just what she did, only the peddler was a practical joker and he informed her that *einnemen a miessa meshuna* meant that you should live a hundred years.

When the manager arrived home, his wife gave him a stern lecture. "Here you go and fire some perfectly noble Jewish man for no good reason. And does he resent it? Does he wish you harm as any normal Christian would do? No! He wishes you a long life and leaves without complaint. You hire that splendid gentleman back immediately, or I'll never speak to you again!"

So the manager called Abe on the phone, and Abe came in for an interview, and the manager asked forgiveness. "Please accept my apologies, Mr. Birnbaum. You are reinstated as of this moment. A noble spirit such as yours must be commended. I hope, too, you and your wife and family will all *einnemen a miessa meshuna.*"

❁ ❁ ❁

Never Marry a Shikse

The story is told that the aged father of George Gershwin, the composer, was once stopped by a motorcycle cop for exceeding the speed limit. After hearing the old man's story, the cop tore up the ticket and went on his way. After all, the old gent had sworn up and down that he was the father of Judge Gershwin, and why ask for trouble down at City Hall?

🌻 🌻 🌻

"Hello, Mr. Goldberg. How's everything?"
"Ehh!"
"And the store—it's making money?"
"Ahh!"
"And Mrs. Goldberg? She's well and happy?"
"Ummmmm—"
"Well, good-bye, Mr. Goldberg. Enjoyed our talk."

🌻 🌻 🌻

Maxie went to visit his cousin Nat in the farm country of New Jersey, where Nat had established a prospering dairy enterprise. Maxie was impressed. Everywhere he saw signs of the latest methods, the most advanced machinery, the most progressive implements of the trade. During a tour through the barn, however, Maxie paused. "Just one thing, cousin Nat," he said apologetically. "These cows—I've never seen this variety in pictures or anywhere. What do you call them?"

"That's easy," said farmer Nat. "They're a cross between a Guernsey and a Holstein. I call them Goldsteins." Just then all the cows looked up in their stalls and *nu*-ed.

🌷 🌷 🌷

Melvin, the butcher, wondered why all the customers kept flocking to Rappaport's, the butcher down the street. So he went to investigate. In the window of Rappaport's he saw a hand-lettered sign: KOSHER BUTCHER. KILLS HIMSELF ONCE A WEEK.

🌷 🌷 🌷

Bessie took a night course in current affairs. Bursting with ideas and information, she ran downtown to see her old *yente* friend Sadie. Over the second glass of tea, Bessie very casually and matter-of-factly asked, "And what is your opinion of Henry Cabot Lodge?"

Quick as a flash, Sadie snapped back, "It's all right—but I like Grossinger's better!"

🌷 🌷 🌷

Mrs. Sternberg called her jet-set attorney to talk business, but the secretary informed her that he had been called to the United Kingdom. "Oh, my," said Mrs. Sternberg, "I'm sorry to hear that. Is it too late to send flowers?"

🌷 🌷 🌷

Sitting around a table on the terrace at the Fontainbleau in Miami, three middle-aged ladies were comparing notes, with a bored air, about the care each gave to her diamond collection. "I send my eight-carat ring to Tiffany's for cleaning," said the first. "Tiffany's?" sniffed the second. "Never heard of it. I have a special messenger who delivers my lavaliere to Mr. Cartier personally. He cleans and polishes it himself." The third lady, Mrs. Simonson, yawned and said, "Such economy you girls practice, I really admire it. When my diamonds get dirty, I throw them in the garbage can!"

The same sort of competitive situation occurs in almost endless variation in urban Jewish lore. The same three ladies (or perhaps it was another trio, not that it makes much difference) once spent an hour or two celebrating the great gifts and achievements of their respective husbands. Said the first, "Vernon is the best provider in the whole world. He not only takes good care of me and the children and all my relatives, but just sent the servants to Europe for a three-week vacation." Said the second, "Well, that's a blessing, but Tobias gives me something a lot more valuable, and that's consideration. He buys me flowers every day of the year, he won't let me do a bit of housework, and he even gives me a shampoo and a manicure." The third lady smiled indulgently, as if she were listening to little children bragging about small matters. "Well, girls, money and consideration are one thing, but my Rodney gives me more happiness than either of you will ever know, and he does it by his sparkling wit. When Rodney's around, I am all smiles and laughter. Just to give an example, last week we went to a nightclub, and Rodney started exchanging remarks with Milton Berle. The audience knew who the real funny man was that night, and Berle was getting angry. Finally he turns to Rodney and says, 'Go home and polish your bald head, old man.' And quick as a flash Rodney says, 'Hoo boy, Uncle Milty, up yours!' That's just what he said, ladies, and got to admit, that's topping Milton Berle."

Then there was the time when the three ladies were bragging about their sons. "Emmanuel is so thoughtful," cooed the first lady. "When he made his first million in the fur business, he had a custom Rolls-Royce made up and delivered as my surprise." Said the second matron, "That's nothing. When Cosmo sold his hotel in Las Vegas, he bought me an island all my own in the St. Lawrence River. Imagine!" Mrs. Margolis, the third lady, brightened up when her turn came. "Spending a lot of money is one thing," she said. "But my Sheldon believes more in the thought that goes into the presents he gives people. For my birthday last year, he toured all over South America just to get me a black peacock. And let me tell you, ladies, it made the most delicious dinner I ever had!"

🌷 🌷 🌷

In Beverly Hills, California, a new variation: "My analyst can lick your analyst!"

And back in New York we have the two Jewish ladies bragging about their rabbis.

"My rabbi is so learned nobody in the whole congregation ever understands a thing he says!" claims Becky.

To which Sadie replies, "Well, that's nothing. You should see *my* rabbi. He's always deep in contemplation, maintaining silence, as he calls it. Ach! Such a silence he maintains! It goes on and on, until it tires him out and he's exhausted!"

Becky is interested despite herself. "So what does he do then?" she wants to know.

"Ah-*ha!*" Sadie answers. "Then he rests for a while, and after he's rested, he maintains silence some more!"

❁ ❁ ❁

In the borough of Queens Izzie Rappaport attended a fancy party thrown by one of his wife's high class friends. When he was introduced to a young Dr. Miller, he drew the fellow aside and proceeded to describe his latest symptoms. "Excuse me, Dr. Miller, but would you mind telling me how I can get over the *tsorres* I get in the *poopik* every morning? It's driving me *meshuggeh,* I have such pain!" Dr. Miller apologized and explained that he was only a recent graduate and that his doctorate was in economics rather than medicine. "Well, why didn't you say so?" beamed Rappaport. "You can tell me whether to sell my General Motors and buy Xerox. And not only that, but I have some real estate in Buffalo and maybe you could advise me if I should. . . ." And so on with Izzie and Dr. Miller.

Meanwhile, back at the Pitkin Avenue movie house in Brooklyn, one of the quiet sentimental scenes in *Funny Girl* was interrupted by the shrill voice of a middle-aged matron calling out from the audience, "Is there a doctor in the house? Please! Is there a doctor in the house?"

Out into the aisle and down to the seat where the cry for help originated steps a smooth well-tailored professional-looking gentleman. "May I help you, madame? I happen to be a physician."

Replies the old lady, "Well, how do you do, Doctor. I'm pleased to make your acquaintance, and how would you like to meet a nice young Jewish girl?"

❀ ❀ ❀

Reb Yossell, who had just passed his eighty-sixth birthday, called in his old doctor friend Chaim Goldman. "Chaim," he told him, "it's my right leg. On rainy days it hurts so bad I can't walk even. I can't get out of bed even."

Dr. Goldman gave the old fellow a thorough examination and then sighed sympathetically. "There's nothing I can do, Reb. It's plainly a case of old age."

But Reb found this hard to accept. "Then how come the left leg is as good as ever?" he demanded.

❀ ❀ ❀

Two fainting victims, a young man and a young lady, were brought into the emergency room for treatment. After they were revived, they told the intern their story. "Well," said the young lady, "I got on the crosstown bus, and it was real crowded, and this young man tipped his hat and got up and offered me his seat. So naturally I fainted dead away."

And what about the young man? the intern wanted to know. "Well," said the young man, "just as I got up to offer her my seat, I heard her say 'Thank you' and that naturally made me grow dizzy and lose consciousness. In short, I swooned."

Business Is Business

AFTER services Rabbi Gerstein came forward and very solemnly addressed the congregation. "I hate to say this, but the membership of this temple is the stingiest in the history of Judaism." A shocked murmur ran the rounds of the seated worshipers. "I've worked faithfully for you going on seven years now," the rabbi continued. "And I still haven't been able to save enough for a down payment on a cheap house. At this moment, my wife needs food for the family, and my children lack clothes to go to school. That is why I chose tonight to bring up this unpleasant subject, because tonight I need one hundred dollars or else!"

The audience held quick private conferences, and finally Moe Weintraub stood up and announced: "Rabbi, everyone here tonight feels embarrassed and ashamed. We have voted to give you one hundred dollars immediately"—the rabbi beamed—"provided you pay us back from your salary check, the one you receive after Passover."

The rabbi consented to the agreement. Then he added reflectively, "If I live until after Passover, that'll be your good luck. And if I die before Passover, believe me, with the cheapskates in this congregation, that'll be my good luck!"

🌸 🌸 🌸

During the Arab-Israeli War of 1967 a minor officer in the Israeli Army broke into the tent of Moshe Dayan, who was involved in an important parley. "Forgive the interruption, Commander," gulped the excited subaltern, "but I have just received dreadful news. A group of Syrian guerrillas has broken into the Bank of Tel Aviv and made off with one million dollars in pledges!"

🌸 🌸 🌸

In the sporting-goods shop of Lefkowitz and Lefkowitz hangs a sign which reads: WE HONOR DINERS' CLUB, MASTER CHARGE, CARTE BLANCHE, AMERICAN EXPRESS, AND MONEY.

🌸 🌸 🌸

When Jack Benny visited the Holy Land a few years ago, he made a point of stopping for a few solemn moments on the shores of the Sea of Galilee. When he was shown the place where according to tradition Christ walked on the water and rendered a powerful sermon,

Benny asked the guide, "How much would a boatman charge to take me all the way across?"

The guide pondered for a moment, then replied, "In American money, ten dollars."

Benny was miffed. "Ten dollars!" he exclaimed. "Now I understand why Jesus walked!"

🌸 🌸 🌸

One evening after a particularly emotional performance the famous actor of the Yiddish stage Boris Tomashevsky started out the stage door on his way home. His progress was blocked by a pathetic, though still attractive, young lady holding a grubby little child in each arm.

"Remember me, Mr. Tomashevsky?" said the girl. "Reba Troublaiavska, your soul mistress for one night of love three years ago."

Tomashevsky grunted a greeting and tried to walk around the young lady.

"Not so fast," she said. "Remember the crazy love we made? Well, these twins are the result of that passionate evening. And I'm all alone in the world with no money. In brief, Mr. Tomashevsky, and to come to the point, we are in dire need, and have no one to turn to."

Tomashevsky was touched. He drew a ticket out of his vest pocket and presented it with his compliments to the troubled young lady.

She stared at it dumbfounded. "A theater ticket to your next performance, Mr. Tomashevsky? What kind of prize is that to offer? These children need bread, do you understand, Mr. Tomashevsky, not tickets, but bread!"

Tomashevsky drew himself up to his full height. "If you want bread, make love to a baker!" he told her with impeccable logic. "Tomashevsky gives tickets!"

🌷 🌷 🌷

In the Southern states sales clerks and store managers have developed a habit of saying to each customer who patronizes their shops, "Thank you. Y'all come back." The formula is more a gesture than a command, and simply expresses appreciation for the customers' patronage. Estes Lazarus, a new Jewish merchant in the town of Columbia, South Carolina, quickly adapted to Southern ways and devised a Southern formula of his own. Whenever somebody bought a suit in his clothing store, Estes would grin and say, "Wear the suit in good health. Wear it a long time, tear it quick, and call again."

🌷 🌷 🌷

Rabbi Swinburne Smolowitz was shocked one day while taking his daily stroll along the boulevard in Miami Beach. There, lolling on the sidewalk was a bum and a beggar, obviously intoxicated and holding up a sign which displayed a Star of David above the legend "Help a poor man." The rabbi walked over and dropped two quarters in the beggar's hand; then stooping over, he addressed the vagabond in a loud, clear voice: "Tell me, my friend, have you no family?"

The beggar looked up and smiled rather foolishly. "Of course I have a family," he slurred.

"Any children, my poor fellow?" asked Rabbi Smolowitz.

"Sure, I got chil'ren," said the beggar. "Five of 'em, and all rich, too."

The rabbi stood erect and gasped in surprise. "Well, in the name of God, why aren't they supporting you?"

The beggar looked hurt and indignant. "Shish—" he said. "Do you think I want to surrender my independence?"

Conrad Scheizdreck was an honest man, and he ran an honest market. When the wholesale fruiterer sold him an order of prunes that were past their prime, Conrad dragged the offending wholesaler before the communal elder, who was noted for his just decisions. For an hour the old man squatted in the marketplace, nibbling away at the questionable prunes. From time to time he seemed on the point of issuing a verdict; then he would hesitate and go back to tasting the prunes. Finally, the elder stood up, adjusted his loincloth, and rendered a statement: "This is ridiculous! What do you take me for, a prune expert!" And he strode away from the marketplace.

Rabbi Shelley Killabendel once advised a frightened Israeli soldier, "Listen carefully, my boy. Don't depend on miracles. Pray a little, too."

Albert Einstein always told his students, "You can recognize an intellectual by the microscope he is looking into." The famous physicist once concluded a scientific lecture by saying, "If my theory of relativity is proved correct, Germany will claim me as a German and France will say I am a citizen of the world. If the theory is proved untrue, France will claim I am a German, while Germany will insist that I am a Jew."

Minnie Guggenheimer was the generous sponsor of the famed Lewissohn Stadium Concerts, which brought her much satisfaction, though also a lot of anxiety about the weather. She once told a reporter that her involvement with the free concerts might be summarized as "forty-four years of blood, sweat, and rain."

Business Is Business

Heinrich Heine said that music played at weddings always reminded him of music played for soldiers before they went off to battle. A believer in Platonic love, the great German-Jewish poet claimed that it helped a man dream by day and sleep by night. Besides, Heine would add, it's so inexpensive.

Heine was paralyzed during the last years of his life and confined to his bed in great pain. Once a friend came to see him and Heine told him, "You can't imagine my suffering. The only thing that keeps me going is the thought that soon I shall die and be released from my suffering. That thought keeps me alive."

❀ ❀ ❀

Benjamin Disraeli opined that when a man falls into his anecdotage, it is time for him to retire.

❀ ❀ ❀

Dr. Chaim Cockinyam, famed pediatrician, feels that the chief advantage of mother's milk is the containers it comes in. "They're so *cute,*" twinkled the physician.

❀ ❀ ❀

In the thirties a bishop of the Russian Orthodox Church was traveling through Germany and stopped to visit an old historic church in a small town. Immediately a crowd of urchins surrounded him and began deriding him for his appearance. The bravest youngster picked up a stone and threw it at the old clergyman. Soon the bishop was in flight down the main street, with a pack of hooting children pelting him with rocks and calling him ugly names.

A Jewish merchant saw the old fellow's predicament and opened the door of his shop as refuge. The bishop dashed in, fell on the floor, and spat out bitter thoughts. "What sort of country is this?" he snorted. "These are not Christians, these boys! They act like heathens—like Jews!"

The merchant helped the old fellow up and could not resist laughing aloud.

"What is so funny?" demanded the irate bishop.

"You would not understand," said the merchant, still laughing. "It would take a thousand years for you to understand."

🌟 🌟 🌟

Israel Zangwill once had an engagement to address a large audience of influential Jews at Albert Hall in London. The trouble, of course, was Zangwill's marriage to a Gentile girl named Edith Ayrton; it had aroused the fury of a great many of Zangwill's associates. Zangwill's wit was equal to the occasion. "Gentlemen," he began, "I know some of you are displeased because I married a

238

Gentile. Yet I trust you will treat my new wife with ulti-
mate courtesy. She deserves your respect, for she married
a Jew."

🌼 🌼 🌼

Abraham Schmucklekopf was married to a lovely girl
and had two lovely children and a lovely apartment on
Riverside Drive. Over on the East Side, Abe had a flashy
mistress, and he was known to be a big investor in the
Saturday-night poker games in Washington Square,
while he was not above helping out with a few shady im-
port deals that somehow got through the New York Port
Authority.

One evening the rabbi called on Abraham and asked
for a donation for the new temple.

"Sorry," said Abe, "but I already gave. I always donate
in secret."

The rabbi looked him squarely in the eye. "Funny,"
he mused out loud. "You sin in secret, and all the congregation knows about it. You give charity in secret, and nobody ever hears a word about it!"

🌼 🌼 🌼

Zero Mostel was the son of a poor rabbi who never neg-
lected to bring home a hungry derelict whenever the
opportunity presented itself. Zero's mother had no
objections to feeding the hungry fellows, but she did

complain about their obviously unwashed condition. "Why can't you ever bring home a *clean* beggar for a change?" she once asked her husband.

"You know why?" he replied. "Because the clean ones the rich get!"

❀ ❀ ❀

As the thirties wore on, most Jewish students disappeared from the public and private schools of Nazi Germany. But Murray, who was in seventh grade, managed to hang on. One day the teacher told the class that Adolf, the Führer, was a great father to them all. "You can be anything with such a father! Let us all say what we would like to be as the children of Adolf!"

So the kids started singing out. "A general of the army!" said one. "A publicity director!" said another. "The captain of the police!" cried a third.

Then the teacher's eyes narrowed as she saw Murray sitting there in silence. "And what would *you* choose to be, as one of Adolf's children?" she asked.

"Oh, that's easy," said Murray. "I'd choose to be an orphan."

A few days later the teacher sent Murray home with a note for his father. "Murray is just like all members of his race," said the note. "He is greedy, pushy, and self-interested. Murray's tuition money totals the amount for just one student, the same as all the others. But is Murray satisfied? No! He has to learn enough for any three of the others!"

❀ ❀ ❀

Sadie was inconsolable. After fifty-five years of marriage, she had just become a widow. She was sitting in her kitchen weeping into her glass of tea, while Shirley, her old friend, tried to cheer her up. "I hate to sound unsympathetic," said Shirley to her disconsolate friend, "but it serves you right. I told you when your married Sam that he had asthma."

❀ ❀ ❀

An Israeli pilot was in trouble. He radioed to the control tower that his wings were full of enemy bullets, his tail control shot away, and his fuel tank perforated. On top of this, his wheels would not descend. "What are my orders?"

The Tell Aviv control man was silent for a moment, then advised solemnly, "Repeat after me. 'I believe with perfect faith in the coming of the Messiah. . . .'"

❀ ❀ ❀

The visiting rabbi had never before addressed a Reform congregation. "What subject shall I lecture on?" he asked the president of the temple. "I thought the sanctity of the Sabbath would be a good topic."

Sterling Lipschitz, the temple president, winced. "No,

no, no!" he said. "That will never do. Almost all our members work on Saturday mornings; you know how it is out here in Long Island—the vacationers and all. Anyway, you'll offend the members."

The visiting rabbi thought awhile and then brightened. "How about *kashruth?*" he asked enthusiastically.

"Don't *say* that word!" Sterling was visibly shaken. "Almost none of our members keep a kosher home!"

The visitor pondered deeply. "What if I speak of the dangers of intermarriage?" he inquired.

"God forbid!" cringed Sterling. "Our most prominent members married Gentile girls. You'd antagonize the whole congregation!"

In desperation, the clergyman threw up his hands. "Well, what *am* I to talk about?" he asked.

Quick as a flash Sterling grabbed him by the arm and propelled him toward the lectern. "Talk about Judaism, of course!" he told the perplexed rabbi.

❀ ❀ ❀

Here's one of my favorite shaggy Martian stories. . . .

An inhabitant of Mars was driving his tiny space vehicle through the cosmos when he spotted Earth and decided to drop down for a visit. As chance would have it, he glided over New York City and landed smoothly on Seventh Avenue around Fifty-seventh Street. As he glided to a stop, the Martian suddenly realized that one of the minuscule tires on his spacecraft had gone flat. He got out of the cabin, investigated, and sure enough, there it was, flatter than a pancake.

Business Is Business

The Martian kicked the offending object in disgust and then looked around. He had come to rest outside the Stage Delicatessen, and his keen eyes immediately spotted a string of bagels hanging in the Stage window. Removing his space gloves and fishing in his pocket for coins, the Martian entered the delicatessen and addressed Al Finklestein, who always sits at the big silver cash register by the door. "How much for one of those wheels in the window?" said the Martian.

Al looked around to see where the piping little voice was coming from. Then he looked down and saw the little silver-suited guy with the antenna growing out of his head. "Wheels?" Al sputtered. "Hey, Ernie!" Al called to his favorite waiter. "Wheels, he wants! Haw, haw, haw!" Then looking down again, Al told the Martian patiently, "Those things in the window are not wheels. They are bagels. You don't ride on them, you eat them."

Now it was the Martian's turn to laugh. "Squeak, squeak, squeak," he laughed. "I don't believe it!" And he carried on that way for two or three minutes. Al finally went over, detached a bagel from the string, cut it open, and gave the Martian a half bagel to chew on.

The Martian took a nibble, looked interested, and took another nibble. Then his face lit up. "Say," he squeaked, "these things would be even better with lox and cream cheese."

🌹 🌹 🌹

Declaun Haun who is as Irish as Jim Farley, Bobby Kennedy, and James Cagney, is also one of the best news

243

photographers. He made the pictures for a *Saturday Evening Post* story on the Presidential campaign of Governor George C. Wallace of Alabama. The photographer stuck pretty close to the segregationist-politician, and during a relaxed moment Haun told Wallace that he had once lived in the South and was familiar with racial segregation, but that he now lived in a Chicago apartment house with a dozen black families and he, his wife, and his children were perfectly at ease and enjoying the fellowship.

The next morning at breakfast, the Alabama governor said, "Haun, I can see why you are happy in Chicago with Negro neighbors—it's because you're Jewish."

🌺 🌺 🌺

The beloved entertainer of the Yiddish and English theater Molly Picon once posed this question:

Can you imagine a woman President of the United States? The Secretary of State rushes into her office and gasps, "Madam President, the Soviets are building up their military strength in Eastern Europe, the Arabs are poised to invade Israel, and two revolutions have just started in South America."

And the lady President answers: "Please, first you'll eat, then you'll talk!"

🌺 🌺 🌺

Business Is Business

A father grew tired of listening to his married son's complaints about his nagging wife. "Don't complain to me about the girl," grumbled the father. "You should have asked for my opinion before you married her, like any respectable Jewish son."

"Did you consult me for my opinion when you got married?" snapped the wrought-up son.

"Now, see here, don't get so fresh with your own father!" roared the older man. "Who needed to ask for your advice? When I got married, it was to your mother. But look what you did—you went and married a perfect stranger!"

🌱 🌱 🌱

MRS. KLEIN: Can you tell if your husband is lying or not, just by looking at his face?
MRS. GROSS: No trouble at all, Mrs. Klein. If his lips are moving, he's lying.

🌱 🌱 🌱

Papa Sol Beson was discussing the careers of his four sons with a friend.

"My oldest son just graduated from medical school," he said, a touch of pride in his voice. The second oldest wants to be an engineer; he's in his second year at MIT. The third wants to be a successful merchant, and he's studying business administration. As for my youngest, he is very spiritual. I think he wants to be a rabbi."

"A rabbi!" cried the neighbor, aghast. "What kind of business is that for a Jew?"

🕎 🕎 🕎

An Israeli bank opened up on Seventh Avenue, New York. In its window was a sign reading: YOU MAY HAVE A FRIEND AT THE CHASE MANHATTAN BANK, BUT HERE YOU'LL FIND GONTZ MESHPACHAH (all of your relatives).

🕎 🕎 🕎

A Jew asked one of his friends who had just returned from the Russo-Japanese War to explain to him how a war is conducted. The other responded: "See that big field? It's like this. We're on one side and they're on the other, and we shoot."

"All day long?" asked his friend.

"All day and all night, too," was the reply.

His friend looked at him quizzically, and said, "But at night, you might hit somebody!"

(*)

🕎 🕎 🕎

Heaven help us

246

Index

Index

Index

Index

Wilson, Woodrow, 139
Wise, Stephen S., 163

Yeshivas, 12
Yezierska, Anzia, 219
Yiddish: development of, 12–
13; press, 13; theater in New

York City, 13; writers, 13–
15, 219 *passim*
Yiddishe Mama, jokes, 69, 81–
86, 92, 97–98, 104–5, 106
Yiddish joke. *See* Jewish joke

Zangwill, Israel, 238